OUTSIDE LIVING

TERRACES, BALCONIES, ROOF DECKS, COURTYARDS,
POCKET GARDENS, AND OTHER SMALL OUTDOOR SPACES

OUTSIDE LIVING

TERRACES, BALCONIES, ROOF DECKS, COURTYARDS, POCKET GARDENS, AND OTHER SMALL OUTDOOR SPACES

FRANCESC ZAMORA MOLA

UNIVERSE

First published in the United States of America in 2015 by
Universe Publishing
A Division of Rizzoli International Publications, Inc.
300 Park Avenue South
New York, NY 10010
www.rizzoliusa.com

Originally published in Spain in 2015 by
Loft Publications S.L.
Domènech 7-9; 2°1ª
08012 Barcelona

2015 2016 2017 2018 / 10 9 8 7 6 5 4 3 2 1

ISBN: 978-0-7893-2918-9

Library of Congress Control Number: 2014957111

Printed in Spain

Editorial coordination: Claudia Martínez Alonso
Art direction: Mireia Casanovas Soley
Edition: Francesc Zamora Mola
Graphic edition: Ana Herrera Moral, Silvia Sánchez Selma
Texts: Aleix Ortuño Velilla, Francesc Zamora Mola, Manel Gutiérrez (@mgutico)
Layout: Cristina Simó Perales, Sara Abril
Translations: Thinking Abroad

Front cover: © Jaime Navarro Soto
Back cover: © Frederico Valsassina Arquitectos, PRO AP

Taking shelter indoors, yet longing for the outdoors is a beautiful paradox that has been confronted by humans since the beginning of time. Men and women learned quickly to take shelter from nature's extremes. Although incipient architecture only served the most basic needs for survival, the connection between home and nature was more than just a dispensable luxury.

Of course, that is no longer the case, as this longing has become unbearable.

It goes without saying that, long ago, architecture overcame the strictly utilitarian phase that originally gave birth to it. Still, the importance of design functionality resurfaces time and time again (as championed by the tenets of minimalism). The architect's task goes far beyond protecting people from the elements; like all spheres of humanity, it has evolved in the same way that gastronomy is no longer solely about providing nutrition but rather transmitting a sensorial experience and medicine is also focused on improving our quality of life rather than only curing diseases. Architecture has also expanded in scope, now striving beyond functionality to provide tranquillity, beauty, and a sense of integration between the building's inhabitants and nature.

Under these circumstances, nature has reclaimed its presence within the home.

What was the cause of this reestablishment? The nexus between nature and home cannot be removed from human beings.

Of course, nature is more than just trees and streams, but also the sky above our heads and the light that reigns over every part of the world. Today, architecture is based on adapting homes to their environments. Buildings must not impose on an environment; rather, they should blend into it on all levels that can be controlled—from choosing the materials to orienting the spaces.

At the same time, sustainable architecture faces increasingly complex challenges because of current issues such as overpopulation and pollution. However, the efforts to overcome these challenges are more active and evident than they have ever been before.

We are at the vanguard of reconnecting nature and architecture.

Indeed, it is that very co existence with nature—where patios, gardens, and balconies have been integrated—that represents the epitome of this connection.

This book has been conceived with the goal of achieving the same immediacy and audacity that defines the gardens sprouting from its pages. There is a system of icons that briefly describes the fundamental roots of each design and the theme observed in the preeminent images. This axis of conceptual coordinates includes, among others, the distinction between a hard surface and a surface with vegetation; the height for patios, gardens, balconies, and terraces, inclusion of water elements, and considerations for positioning the building.

The gardens, balconies, terraces, and patios that are included in this book may stem equally from rural contexts as well as urban. Their function is the same in both types of environments: to go beyond the frontiers of the once-impenetrable concept of the home.

We often imagine the future as one of untethered urbanism. The somber images provided by science fiction make us believe in the idea that Earth might possibly one day be covered only with buildings, like one uninterrupted city. We associate these nearly-mythical musings with the worst aspects of urbanism: overpopulation, pollution, and darkness, which is akin to placing obstacles in front of the sunlight.

Taking a more sensible approach to the way that the world's natural spaces are preserved is a human responsibility and must be part of our ever-increasing commitment to environmentalism. Besides, we have no other choice. Overpopulation is a problem that is as real as it is apparently unsolvable, and is leading us to a future in which the inhabitants of urbanized areas must face brutal overcrowding.

Despite this darkness that we fear, a glimmer of hope has emerged from what has already been achieved. In the present world, where environmental circumstances are adverse, landscapers find that technology, materials, and water reuse are among the key architectural elements to maintaining green spaces and the volume of outdoor space, as well as bringing nature into the deepest parts of the city.

Fusing nature and architecture invites optimism; this book represents a commemoration of this fusion.

The following pages are the sunlight entering into each home, one window after another.

Urban environment

Rural environment

Bottom level

Middle level

Top level

Vertical garden

Interior courtyard

Outdoor area

Hard surfaces

Green area

Water element

ARMADALE RESIDENCE

MELBOURNE, VIC, AUSTRALIA

Architect // Lewis Marash

Photographer // © Dean Bradley

Out From The Blue is a company that specializes in building patios and terraces, with a particular emphasis on swimming pools. With the same dedication that an architecture firm devotes to building an entire house, OFTB creates pools that stand out for more than simply their shape and size. "The most important thing about a pool is its location," says Marash. At the end of the day, some pools do more than simply invite you to dive in; they invite you to immerse your entire gaze in them. So carefully positioned next to a lounge or dining room, a pool can be enjoyed by its owners every day of the year —an object of art created from water.

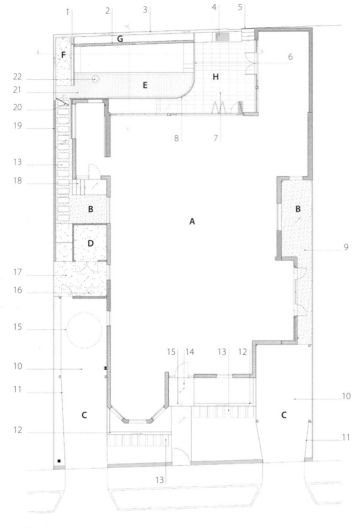

A. Residence
B. Courtyard
C. Garage
D. Storage/Shed/Utilities
E. Pool deck
F. Service yard
G. Garden bed

1. Masonry block work feature wall with stone cladding on face
2. Top of tiled pool beam
3. Masonry block work wall
4. BBQ bench with built-in BBQ and storage. On site concrete bench top and sides, polished finish
5. SHS steel sliding gate with CFC sheet cladding on both sides
6. EZF glazing channel for frameless glass pool fence
7. Porcelain tile
8. Channel in paving to accommodate frameless glass pool fence and gate. Paving to extend 100 mm under timber deck
9. Gravel infill
10. Exposed aggregate concrete paving, wash off finish
11. 200 mm x 1000 mm x 30 mm bluestone tile
12. Masonry block work garden edge, cement render finish
13. 800 mm x 400 mm bluestone pavers with gravel
14. 100 mm x 300 mm x 30 mm bluestone tile, sawn
15. 10,000 liters in ground water tank
16. Dynabolt fold-out clothesline to back of garage wall
17. Natural gray concrete, steel float finish
18. 64 mm x 19 mm spotted gum timber deck
19. (E) rendered block work wall, paint finish
20. SHS steel gate with timber batten cladding to match exterior wall of house (pool side only)
21. Timber sunbathing deck
22. 500 mm diameter. Hole in deck for proposed canopy tree

Site plan

The brief from the client was for a low maintenance garden with an architectural look, but most importantly they wanted the pool to be as large as possible without being disproportionate to the space.

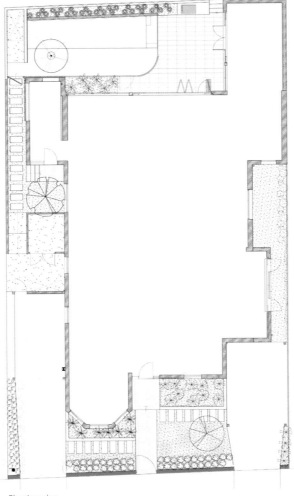

Planting plan

Acer palmatum 'Bloodgood'

Elaeocarpus reticulatus

Ficus microcarpa

Fraxinus griffithii

Robinia pseudoacacia

Agave attenuata
Ajuga reptans 'Caitlin's Giant'
Carex 'Frosted curls'

Doryanthes excelsa
Liriope 'Evergreen giant'
Parthenocessus tricuspidata

Phyllostachys nigra
Strelitzia reginae
Trachelospermum asiaticum
Yucca filamentosa

COURTYARD

Bluestone tile detail (front)

1. 100 mm x 300 mm bluestone tile 20 mm thick
2. 20 mm mortar layer, 4:1 sand/cement
3. Concrete base minimum 100–150 mm. thick
4. Fully compacted subgrade/crushed rock

1. Paving mortar, and concrete subbase
2. Frameless glass fence
3. Channel to be filled with non shrink grout and corked where necessary
4. Rubber packing grommet

Frameless glass attachment detail

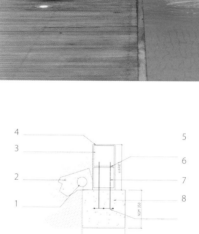

Exposed aggregate concrete detail

1. 100 mm depth 25 MPa concrete
2. F82 mesh centrally placed
3. Minimum 50 mm depth compacted class 2a crushed rock
4. Fully compacted subgrade

Block work retaining wall/garden edge

1. 90 mm diameter agricultural pipe connect to storm water
2. ½ screenings
3. Block course
4. Garden side of wall to be tanked with waterproof membrane. Other surfaces to be prepared for stone cladding.
5. Mortar
6. Starter bars
7. Footing to solid ground
8. 3 bar TM 11

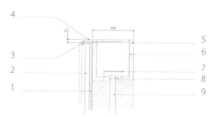

Water wall through detail

1. Render wall to create smooth surface for granite
2. 300 mm x 600 mm x 20 mm granite tile
3. Stainless steel C section
4. Cut top block at front so that height at rear of wall prevents water overflow
5. Nominal 390 mm x 190 mm 190 mm lintel/bond beam as water trough
6. Seal interior of top block with render and membrane
7. 3 mm stainless steel cover over pipe to diffuse water flow
8. HydraTite® tape
9. 25 mm PVC pipe

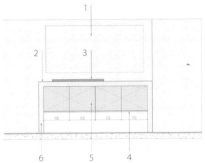

Built-in BBQ and cabinetry

1. Block work wall
2. On-site concrete bench top, polished finish
3. Built-in BBQ in concrete bench top
4. Base of storage cabinets to be 18 mm thick CFC sheet
5. Cabinet doors to be 12 mm CFC sheet paneling
6. On-site concrete "legs" of bench to be 90 mm thick, polished finish

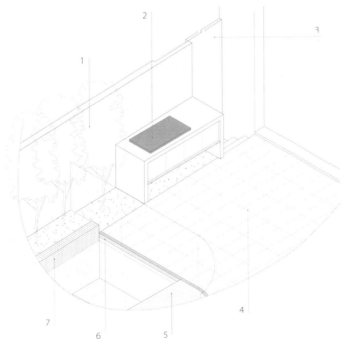

Outdoor dining/built-in fireplace and rear access

1. Garden bed planting
2. BBQ bench with built-in BBQ and storage, on-site concrete bench top and sites, polished finish
3. SHS steel sliding gate with CFC sheet cladding on both sides
4. 300 mm x 600 mm porcelain tile
5. 30 mm x 19 mm spotted gum timber deck
6. Rebate on edge of pool shell to accommodate EZF glazing channel, in which frameless glass pool fence panels are fixed
7. Raised pool wall. Pool tile to wrap up and over wall to garden bed on opposite side.

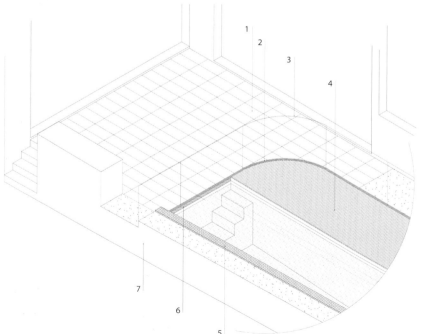

1. Outdoor dining, 300 mm x 600 mm porcelain tile
2. Channel in paving to accommodate frameless glass pool fence and gate
3. Custom curved frameless glass
4. 30 mm x 19 mm spotted gum timber deck
5. Raised pool wall. Pool tile to wrap up and over wall to garden bed on opposite side.
6. EZF glazing channel, in which frameless glass pool fence panels are fixed
7. Masonry block work retaining wall and boundary fence

Pool deck/fence and outdoor dining

It was particularly important for the designers to consider how to fence the pool without it being intrusive to the entertaining area outside of the pool space.

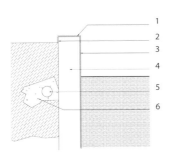

Raised pool wall

1. Mortar
2. Garden side of wall to be tanked with water proof membrane
3. Pool tiles
4. Pool shell
5. 90 mm diameter agricultural pipe connected to storm water
6. ½ screenings

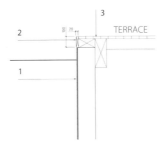

Timber deck and fascia

1. Pool tile face to finish flush with timber fascia as shown
2. Finish decking with 55 mm x 19 mm fascia pieces with 10 mm spacer. Face of timber and tile to finish flush as shown.
3. Decking substructure to be clad with 60 mm. x 19 mm spotted gum timber battens with minimal spacing

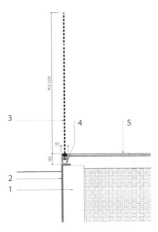

Pool fascia and glass pool fencing

1. Pool shell
2. Pool tile
3. Frameless glass fence panels
4. Custom-made stainless steel channel
5. Porcelain tile

MIDDLEPARK RESIDENCE

MELBOURNE, VIC, AUSTRALIA

Architect // **Lewis Marash**

Photographer // © **Dean Bradley**

Attempting to draw the pool into the warmth of the home, right into its very lounge, required daring moves such as knocking down walls. This is one of the hallmarks of Out From The Blue—glass panels that enable us to see beneath the surface of the water from the comfort of the sofa. So the pool becomes another room of the house, a room that may be costly to maintain, but which bestows an unmatchable aura of exoticism on the rest of the house.

This project is not only striking in terms of the pool design but also in terms of the role of the pool in the spatial composition of the landscape as a whole.

Southwest elevation

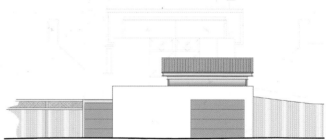

Northeast rear boundary elevation

Capitalizing on the change in floor level of the building, the combined living, dining, and kitchen area is sunken between the pool and the pond courtyards.

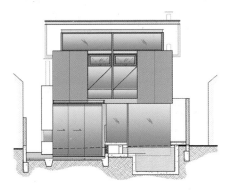

Section A-A

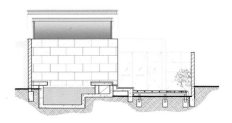

Section B-B

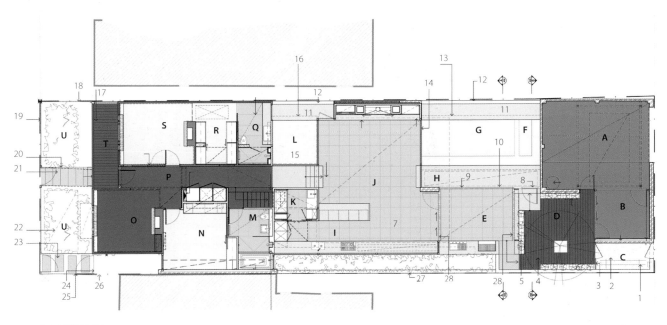

Ground floor plan

A. Garage
B. Multi-purpose room
C. Drying court
D. Podium
E. Outdoor BBQ area
F. Spa
G. Pool
H. Elevated path
I. Kitchen
J. Living/dining area
K. Laundry room
L. Reflective pool patio
M. Bathroom
N. Guestroom/Study
O. Sitting room
P. Hallway
Q. En-suite bathroom
R. Dressing room
S. Master bedroom
T. Veranda
U. Garden

1. Clotheslines
2. Loose pebbles finish
3. Metal gate and side screen
4. Podium timber decking
5. Planter box
6. Garden bed
7. Stone tiles
8. 1,200 mm high frameless glass pool gate
9. 1,200 mm high glass balustrade
10. Metal framed 40 mm x 20mm battened timber access panel under for pool cover maintenance
11. Concrete screed finish
12. Rendered masonry fence
13. Pool extent under
14. Glazed pool wall
15. Reflective pool at living room level, 300 mm maximum pool depth

16. Alignment of water feature spillway under
17. (N) timber veranda floor
18. (E) side picket fence to remain
19. (N) timber picket fence with timber posts and Victorian metal caps
20. Line up with wall
21. Basalt paved entry path
22. 12,000 liters modular water retention tank
23. Basalt stepping stone in landscape
24. (N) picket screen fence
25. (E) side picket fence to remain
26. (E) neighboring timber screen
27. Masonry boundary wall
28. Steel channel drain and grate

FLOOR FINISHES

	Screed
	Carpet
	Timber
	Stone
	Water
	Concrete

	(E) structure
	Proposed structure

MOOLOOMBA
HOUSE

POINT LOOKOUT, STRADBROKE ISLAND,
AUSTRALIA

Architect // Shaun Lockyer Architects
Photographer // © Scott Burrows

This puzzle-inspired house needs a central courtyard to anchor it to the ground. The capricious and colorful construction orbits around it in a series of pavilions, which has its own function. The house needed to be fun as its owners wanted it as a place to escape from the city, a sanctuary just 200 meters from the sea, where they could renounce the monotony of the weekly grind. For this to work, the courtyard and the building's surroundings must be up to the challenge. They are. The house does not close in on itself, nor is it diluted by its views to the outside.

This house explores the organic evolution of the "Straddle Shack" in a contemporary vernacular, consisting of a series of distinct pavilions around an east-facing courtyard.

East elevation

South elevation

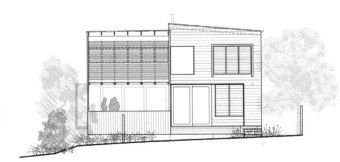

North elevation

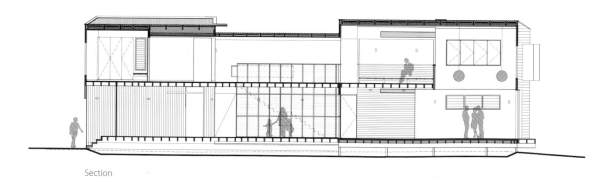

Section

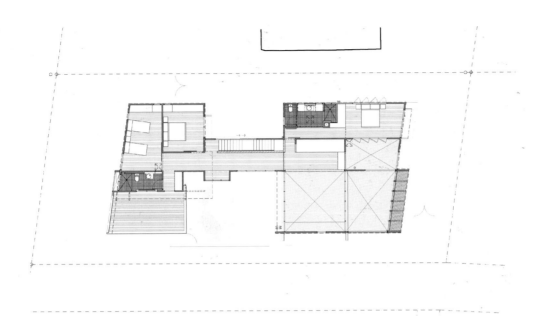

Second floor plan

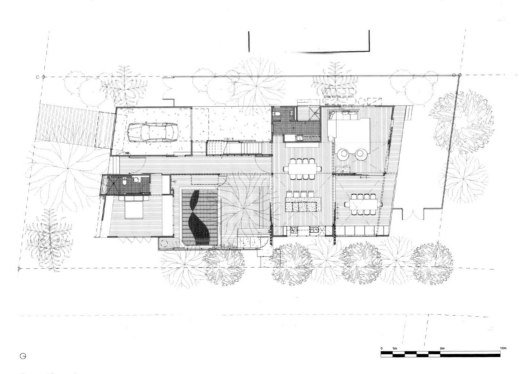

Ground floor plan

The courtyard breaks down the scale of the house and opens the spaces up to the easterly breezes, draws in the sun, and creates a secluded retreat from the adjacent street.

BROOKLYN HEIGHTS TOWN HOUSE

BROOKLYN, NY, USA

Architect // **SPG Architects**

Landscape architect // **Robin Key Landscape Architecture**

Photographer // © **Peter Murdock**

This five-story town house was built in 1836 and everything about it, right through to the garden, is a juxtaposition of tradition and modernity that results from the use of the latest technology and contemporary architecture in a nineteenth-century building. Using art as a leitmotif throughout the house, together with color and finishes for cohesion, the garden feels completely integrated into the building. This helps to remind us that despite the fact that it has no walls or ceiling, a garden is nonetheless an architectural object.

The owners are Sharon and Maxine, an artist whose works are acclaimed in the United States and Europe. One of her sculptures is in the garden. The house is not a product of the architects, but rather it reflects its owners.

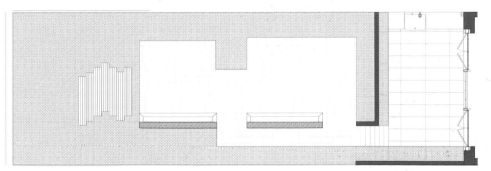

Backyard floor plan

The garden is an extension of the kitchen: as easy as bringing together the tiles on the floor to connect the inside and out. People crave fresh air—all the better from the comfort of their own homes.

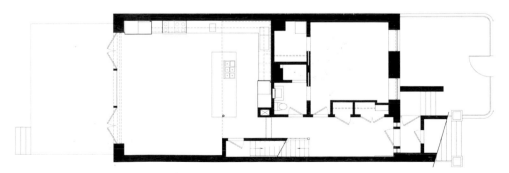

House floor plan

TITLIS GARDEN

ZURICH, SWITZERLAND

Architect // **ArchitekturBureau Garzotto**
Landscape architect // **Fletcher Studio**
Photographer // **© Bruno Helbling**

The green pools and rugged design set out to simulate an authentic mountain river in the garden of this house. The water is neither transparent nor crystalline—in other words it is not artificial. It is pure, however, in a more radical and authentic way—a self-sustaining pool, which needs no chemicals and which is inextricably linked to nature, to the presence of dragonflies, amphibians, and birds. It renounces sterility to provoke a reaction and the result is far-reaching.

Site plan

Titlis garden is located on a steep forested site below an existing house. The site conditions required the construction of retaining walls, which become the dominant feature of this design.

Gabion walls organize this outdoor space consisting of a biopool, a Jacuzzi, a fully equipped kitchen, and a pergola with retractable shading and overhead infrared heating.

MOLTZ
LANDSCAPE

TUCSON, AZ, USA

Architect // Ibarra Rosano Design Architects

Photographer // © Bill Timmerman

Here we witness the classic confrontation between chaotic nature and the human will to establish order and straightness. Random shapes occur even in the strict monotony of the desert, in this case trees growing haphazardly around the house. The garden was built with complete respect for its untamed natural environment, yet brought its own sense of rational distribution to the ensemble. The concrete compartmentalizes and brings order to the desert surface, to this strange combination of vegetation and void. As the Ibarra Rosano team say, "architecture is fundamentally about space."

A double cantilever concrete wall is the first thing to greet you on arrival. Through a doorless entrance, the main access, you are directed to the courtyard via a dry stonewall.

The courtyard design is displayed in horizontal planes of colored concrete. The concrete slabs create planters, benches, and outdoor spaces that rest gently on the desert floor.

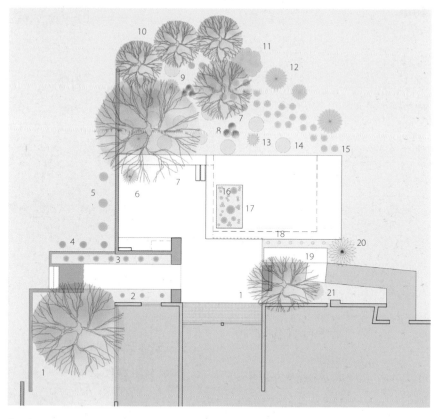

Site plan

1. *Parkinsonia microphylla*
2. *Opuntia subulata*
3. *Echinocactus grusoni*
4. *Dasylirion wheeleri*
5. *Pachycereuse shottii monstrosus*
6. *Yucca gloriosa*
7. *Rhus lancea*
8. *Opuntia violacea*
9. *Dioon edule*
10. *Chilopsis linearis*
11. *Nerium oleander*
12. *Yucca carnerosa*
13. *Ferocactus wislizeni*
14. *Variegated agave americana*
15. *Euphorbia lathyris*
16. *Pachycereus marginatus*
17. *Zephyranthes*
18. *Senecio mandraliscae*
19. *Aloe ferox*
20. *Agave americana*
21. *Yucca glauca*

HOUSE IN SAVYON

SAVYON, ISRAEL

Architect // **Alex Meitlis**

Photographer // © Yael Pincus

This labyrinth of walls, with different openings that direct light in unique ways and produce their own shadows, blurs the distinction between house and garden. They are all rooms, some with roofs, some without, and others partially open. This also serves a practical purpose in dealing with a climate that changes throughout the year. The sun provides light and warmth in winter, but not at the expense of completely exposing the house and leaving it at the mercy of the sun's rays during a hot, dry summer. The practicalities seem less important, however, than the sleepy, hypnotic aura that envelops the house.

Elevations and sections

Gardens, open spaces, and pool occupy three quarters of this project site. In this space, high walls divide the different environments and create alternative routes for natural light.

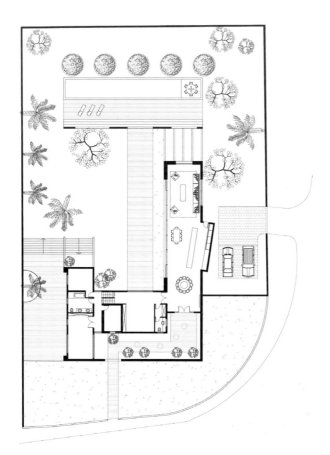

Ground floor plan

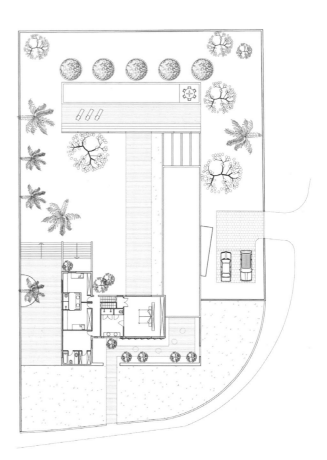

Second floor plan

Every room in the house opens to an adjacent terrace and landscaped area: the windows, like frames for their natural environment, foster a close dialogue between outside and inside.

MAXIMUM MINIMUM SPACE

POZUELO DE ALARCÓN, MADRID, SPAIN

Landscape architect // GM3 Estudio de Paisajismo

Photographer // © Miguel Moreno Mateos

This unique patio adjacent to a dwelling is organized in two spaces: an outdoor living area and a pool area. A vertical garden stands out as the most prominent feature of the patio and frames the pool along one of its long sides. This green decorative element, along with plantings that fill the space, softens the harshness of wall and pavement finishes, contributing to the creation of a pleasant and relaxing environment. At the same time, the planted sections of the patio are used as organizers of the space, separating different uses. This design solution favors a softer transition between areas as opposed to fences and grilles, which offer a more rigid layout and connection between spaces.

The courtyard space is visually divided into two parts by a Magnolia × soulangeana lattice plant, allowing the living area and pool to be enjoyed independently.

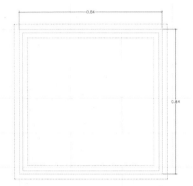

Plan of outdoor shower pan

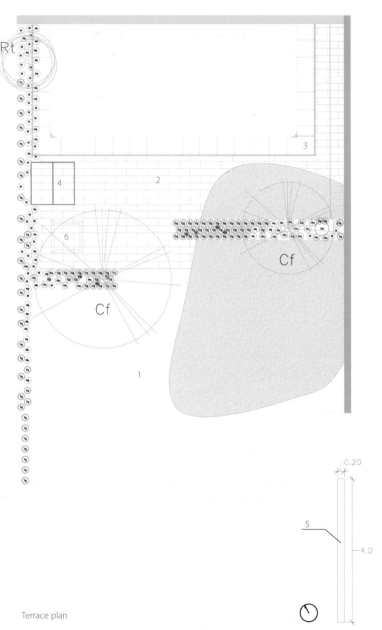

Terrace plan

1. Non slip continuous pavement of white sand, epoxy finish
2. Sierra Elvira stone pavers, 20 mm thick, running bond
3. Sierra Elvira stone pool coping
4. Access hatch to pool equipment
5. Herb garden
6. Outdoor shower

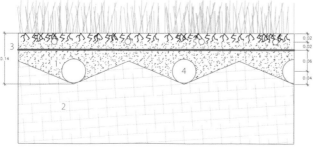

Drainage and irrigation detail

1. Washed gravel for drainage
2. Natural ground
3. Geotextile separation layer between drainage and irrigation systems
4. Drainage pipe DN 65
5. Rain Bird® XFD2333200 irrigation system

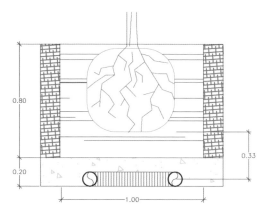

Tree planting detail

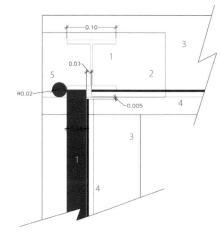

Bushes and plants planting detail

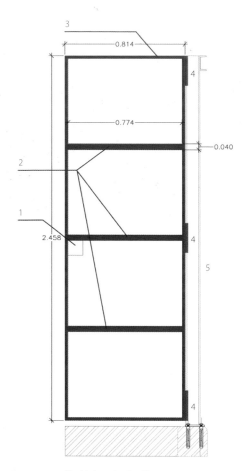

Steel tube gate elevation

1. Lock
2. Steel tube 40 mm x 40 mm
3. Steel tube 40 mm x 200 mm
4. Hinge welded to steel tube
5. Steel angle HEB

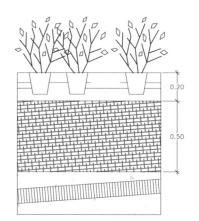

Plan detail at garden gate and Prodema® fence

1. Steel angle HEB
   100 mm x 100 mm
2. Steel plate 10 mm thick
3. Concrete footing
4. Prodema® panel glued
   with Sikaflex® adhesive
5. Steel hinge

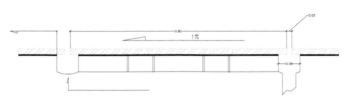

Section through outdoor shower pan

The harmonious combination of traditional materials, such as Sierra Elvira marble, and contemporary ones, such as the wood composite enclosure, creates a warm and functional environment.

NORRA VRAM

NORRA VRAM, BJUV, SWEDEN

Architect // **Marge Arkitekter**

Photographer // © Johan Fowelin

This nineteenth-century Swedish mansion was rebuilt as a nursing home and needed the outdoor spaces to work. So the architects gave the building the appearance of an old Swedish farm, providing access to the garden or to an interior courtyard from every corner. It considers nature as a therapeutic influence, and long, narrow corridors as a necessary evil to be avoided, given that they can make a place such as this feel dungeon like. Instead, this residence becomes one big meeting point, close to the elements.

A. Lobby
B. Residents' rooms
C. Hallways
D. Courtyard
E. Living/dining room
F. Visitors room
G. Kitchen
H. Open office

Floor plan

The design of this nursing home reflects its need to address particular concerns: scale, visual contact between residential and common spaces, and the integration of greenery for health benefits.

HOUSE IN NISHIMIKUNI

NISHIMIKUNI, YODOGAWAKU,
OSAKA PREF., JAPAN

Architect // arbol
Photographer // © Yasunori Shimomura

The paradox of a family house located in the heart of the city is undoubtedly full of challenges. Among these is privacy, especially if you do not want to compromise on sunlight. This house was built for a retired couple and is laid out over a single floor. Within it, courtyards serve as more than simple vehicles for providing light to the space—they are a refuge of fresh air between the buildings. This house does not need to be five floors high nor reach over all the available land in the neighborhood. The empty space and circularity of the garden make it limitless.

Dwarfed by tall adjacent buildings, this house is kept private by a wooden fence, which also brings a natural touch to the property, in contrast with the gray and polluted urban surroundings.

Floor plan

South elevation

East elevation

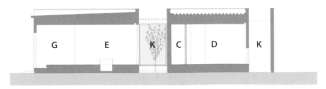

Section A

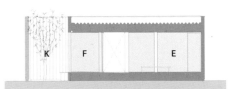

Section B

A. Parking
B. Entrance
C. Storage
D. Bedroom
E. Living/Dining
F. Tatami
G. Kitchen
H. W/C
I. Lavatory
J. Bathroom
K. Garden

A narrow deck cantilevers over the ground, bringing out a sense of lightness. Despite the reduced dimensions of the property, the gardens make the property less confined, adding to comfort.

The gardens add another level of separation between the house and the fence that encircles it. The gardens are narrow strips of planting beds and gravel, enough to evoke a sense of calm.

SAN-SEN HOUSE

VALLE DE BRAVO, MEXICO

Architect // **Alejandro Sánchez García Arquitectos**

Photographer // © **Jaime Navarro Soto**

This house is suspended by a steel structure and anchored to the ground by the stone tower. It may seem excessive artifice, but locating a house on such a unique surface as this untamed forest bed required such treatment. The result was worth it. The hierarchical relationship between house and garden twists and changes so that the end result is not a house that looks out onto a garden, but an unlimited garden (the forest itself) that looks onto a house.

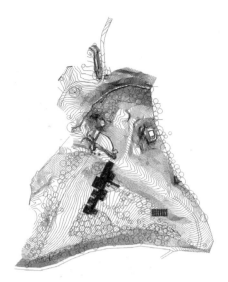

Site plan

This project is based on a steel structure that floats above the ground. It is lined with wood and glass, and the construction allows for spaces to be opened up or closed off in line with the views.

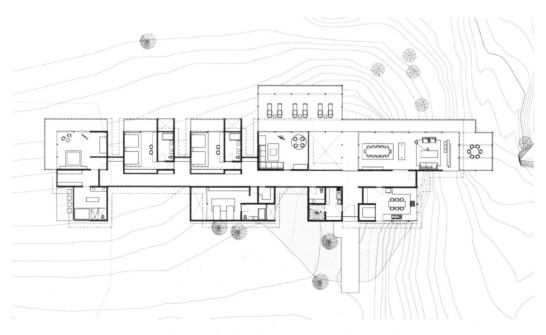

Floor plan

Through a series of courtyards, pavilions, and well-lit interiors, the house exudes an aura of sophistication and elegance that is rare in the heart of a wooded setting.

ONE WYBELENNA

BROOKFIELD, BRISBANE, AUSTRALIA

Architect // **Shaun Lockyer Architects**
Landscape architect // **BOSS Gardenscapes**
Photographer // © Scott Burrows

This house was developed out of the remains of a cottage by Robin Gibson that existed on the site. Its linear plan with rooms oriented to benefit from sun exposure during the winter allows easy access to the pool and the garden making the most of outdoor living during the summer. The structural method, the integration of stone masonry, and the landscape design are key aspects of the overall design made evident by stone blades bisecting the house and delineating interior and exterior zones. The strong sustainable character of the house features green roofs, rainwater tanks, solar panels, and recycled materials including stone and timber.

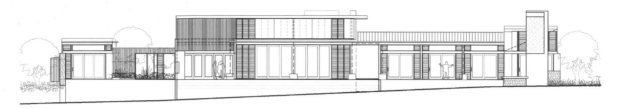

North elevation

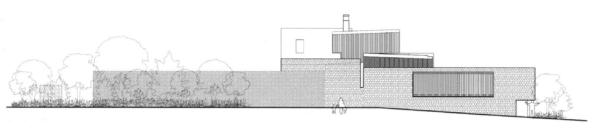

East elevation

South elevation

West elevation

The spacious garage roof is entirely covered with grass, propagating the idea of the house being an integral part of the adjacent land.

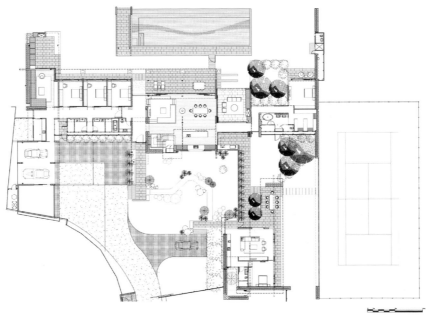

Ground floor plan

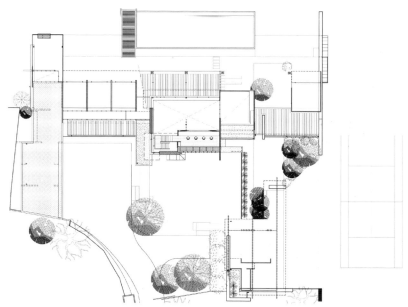

Second floor plan

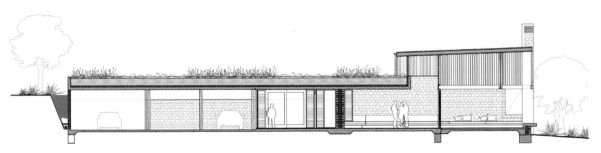

Section

A pool, 25 meters in length, is used to define the northern boundary of the property. This in turn frames the spectacular outdoor living areas.

OUTRIAL HOUSE

KSIAZENICE, POLAND

Architect // **Robert Konieczny ı KWK Promes**
Photographer // © **Juliusz Sokolowski**

A clearing in a dense forest is the backdrop of this singular house with the living quarters on the lower floor and a recording studio on the upper floor. Its architectural language responds to the requirement to integrate the house with its natural surrounding and reflects a strong conceptual design. A piece of the property is cut out to insert the house in its place. Then, this piece of land is put back on top of the house to serve as a green roof. The design is further developed by cutting a "tongue" out of the green roof and bending it down to create an atrium, which, in addition to allowing light and air into the lower floor, is the main access to the house.

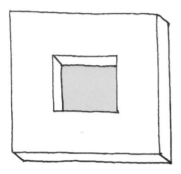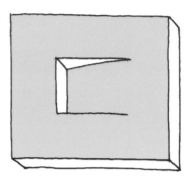

Conceptual diagrams

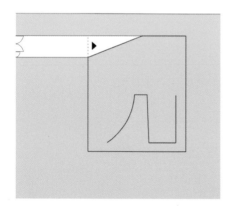

Roof plan

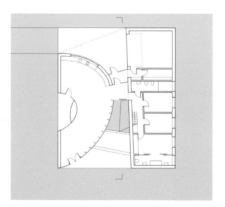

Ground floor plan

With exquisite confusion between floor and ceiling and greenery camouflaging the house, the architects emphasize the atrium. An atypical atrium that rises from patio to ceiling, it resembles a work by M. C. Escher.

The grass could not be lost: it rose and became a roof instead. The atrium followed suit, and the client gained a courtyard that he would convert into a music studio.

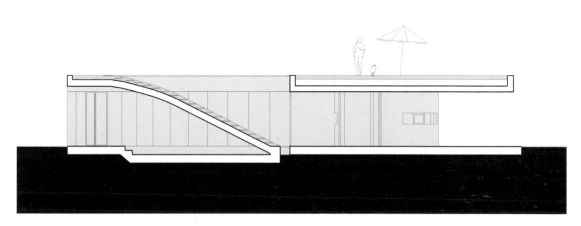

Section

TWO SINGLE FAMILY DWELLINGS

LUQUE, PARAGUAY

Architect // **Bauen**

Photographer // © Marcelo Jiménez and Monica Matiauda

This meadow stretched away like a blank canvas onto which any construction could have been projected, but the architects opted for a more unusual option—to try to leave the canvas blank. The lawn that rises over the roof is both aesthetic, thanks to its embellishment, and functional in its role as an excellent thermal insulator. But it is neither of these features that distinguishes the home—it is its unnerving visual impact. A house with the land on its roof cannot help but create surprise.

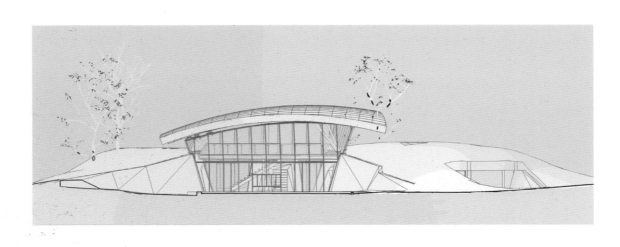

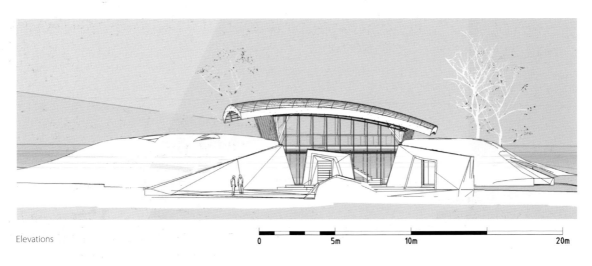

Elevations

0   5m   10m   20m

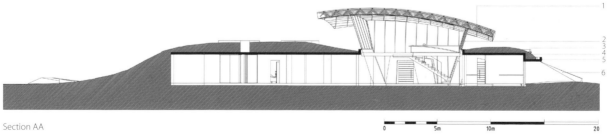

Section AA

1. Lightweight concrete finish over expanded sheet metal, over steel structure
2. Steel framed windows
3. Waterproof insulation layer
4. Grass covered embankment
5. Reinforced concrete slab
6. Stone wall

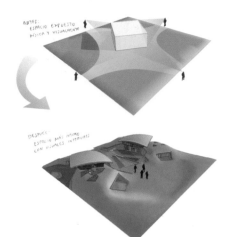

Conceptual design diagram

Green shelter is an interpretation of the typical rural construction in Paraguay. It is a bioclimatic solution belonging to the region's traditional way of living in harmony with the natural environment.

CONTINUIDAD VERDE COMO VISTA EXTERIOR

ESPACIO INTERIOR RESGUARDADO

CONTINUIDAD VERDE COMO VISTA EXTERIOR

Conceptual design diagram

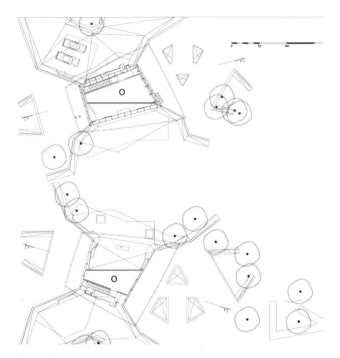

Second floor plan

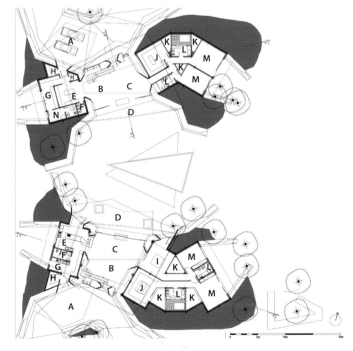

A. Garage
B. Dining room
C. Living room
D. Deck
E. Kitchen
F. Powder room
G. Laundry room
H. Storage
I. TV room
J. Dressing room
K. Patio
L. Bathroom
M. Bedroom
N. Utility room
O. Office

Ground floor plan

The original space of vegetation displaced by construction is recovered with the creation of green roofs. Vegetation-covered roofs mitigate the heat island effect.

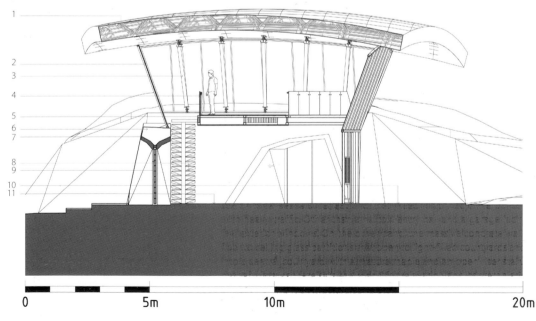

1. Lightweight concrete
   finish over expanded
   sheet metal, over
   steel structure
2. Steel framed windows
3. Steel tube
4. Steel and
   glass guardrail
5. Floor assembly:
   hardwood flooring over
   steel structure
6. Stone wall
7. Reinforced
   concrete portico
8. Steel and wood stair
9. Wood door
10. Recycled wood deck
11. Porcelain tile

0   5m   10m   20m

Section BB

Not only do green roofs reduce the visual and physical impact on the natural environment, they also reduce heat transfer and provide sound insulation to improve indoor comfort.

LOOKOUT HOUSE

GUAYLLABAMBA, ECUADOR

Architect // **Francisco Almeida, Tatiana Bohorquez | AR+C**
Photographer // © **Lorena Darquea**

Located on a hillside, this house and viewing platform penetrate the earth as though it were a den that had found its way into our world. The house arouses sensations that reach beyond our curiosity about its proposition, sensations that encompass the ecological focus of the entire project. The greenery is not just for show, it has a meaning, as does the name of the architects who designed it: AR+C stands for "archquitectura con conciencia" (architecture with conscience).

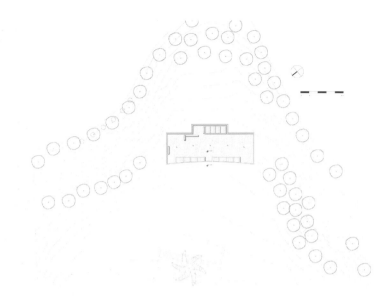

Site plan

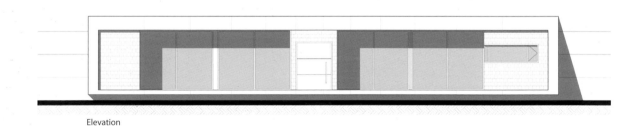

Elevation

Section B-B

This family home, designed to be embedded within the mountain, is a continuation of its natural environment and preserves the pre-construction qualities of the location as a viewing point.

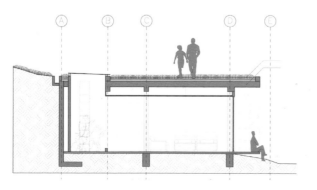

Section A-A

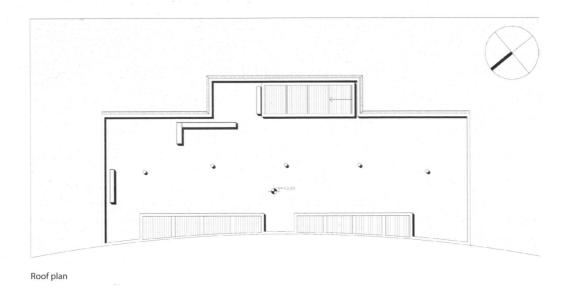

Roof plan

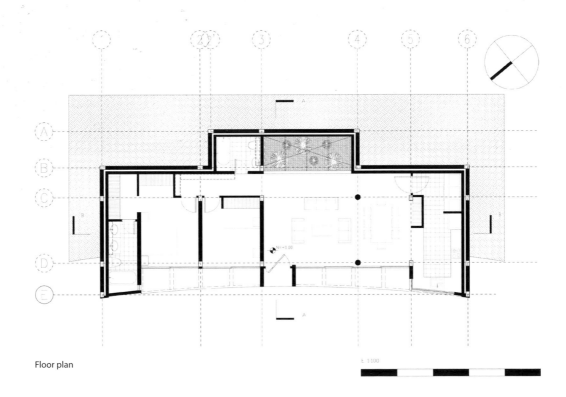

Floor plan

The structure can hold up to 20 cm of vegetation on the roof. The skylights are opened from inside, providing cross ventilation and a link from the house to the deck.

BEACH HOUSE AT PUNTA VELEROS

LOS ÓRGANOS, PERU

Architect // **Artadi Architects**

Photographer // © Elsa Ramírez

Creating a house with an overgrown roof is a way of assimilating the building with the carob tree that dominates the foreground and draws in the natural environment that surrounds it, according to the architects. This platform onto the marine landscape changes it from being "a house on the beach" to "a beach house" in a very honest way. This building invites you to enjoy the beach from the terraces, as though you had walked right down to the water's edge and buried your feet in the sand.

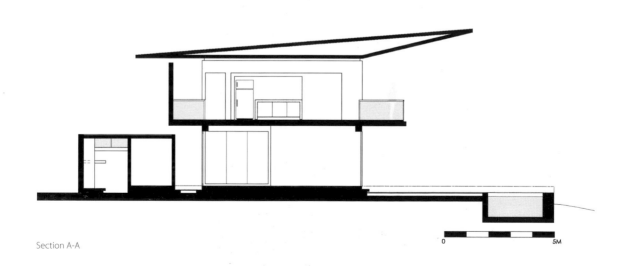

Section A-A

0   5M

This property is a showcase of desert seascape in which a solid form decomposes—a tray holding a social area, which is visually projected onto the horizon.

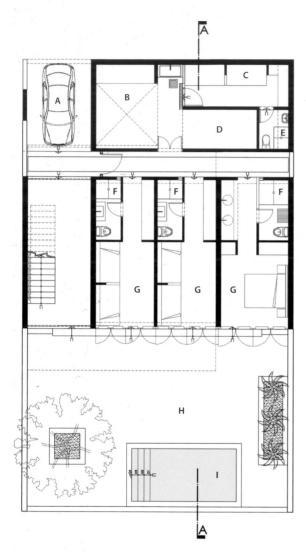

Ground floor plan

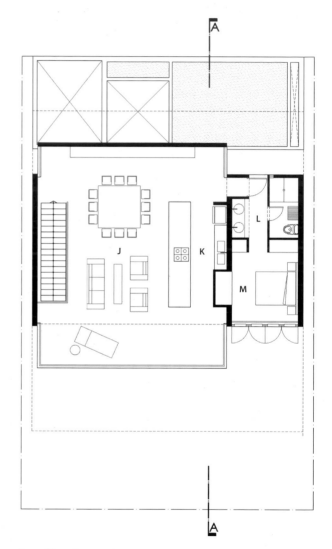

Second floor plan

A. Garage
B. Patio
C. Staff bedroom
D. Storage
E. Staff bathroom
F. Bathroom
G. Bedroom
H. Terrace
I. Pool
J. Living/dining room
K. Kitchen
L. Master bathroom
M. Master bedroom

BEACH WALK HOUSE

FIRE ISLAND, NY, USA

Architect // **SPG Architects**

Landscape architect // **Robin Key Landscape Architecture**

Photographer // © **Daniel Levin**

The strict building regulations of the area—including building height, setbacks and site coverage, the proximity of neighboring houses, and very specific view corridors—presented a host of challenges that conditioned the architectural design. As a result, the house is a two-story structure, rotated off the prevailing grid, and composed of three intersecting volumes of different proportions and finishes. The overall composition generates a series of interior and exterior spaces maximizing both views and privacy. The wood siding of the two lower volumes echoes the surrounding natural colors, while the metallic cladding of the upper volume reflects the landscape made of sand dunes.

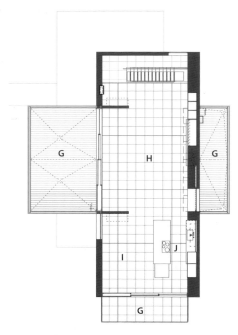

Second floor plan

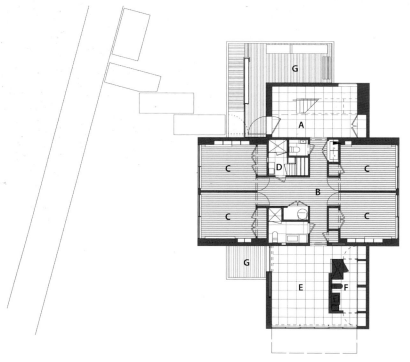

A. Entrance
B. Hall
C. Bedroom
D. Bathroom
E. Master bedroom
F. Master bathroom
G. Deck
H. Living room
I. Dining room
J. Kitchen

Ground floor plan

Each part of the house has a purpose. Here, the roof of one section forms the terrace of the section above. In this case minimalism is not just an aesthetic but a philosophy, too.

The ocean is across the dunes from this beach house, which has been designed with storage for water sports equipment. The garden is integrated into the landscape above the sea.

PRIVATE GARDEN

FORCH, SWITZERLAND

Landscape architect // DARDELET

Photographer // © DARDELET

A haven of peace. The owner of this house is a surgeon, who had asked the architects to create a place where he could relax after long, high-pressure days at work, and where his wife and three children could enjoy a healthy lifestyle. The building is the epitome of space, silence, and nature (the latter enclosed in the courtyards as though it were jars of oxygen), all drawing on the sound-proofing of the entire structure. A modern temple for a relaxed but everyday existence.

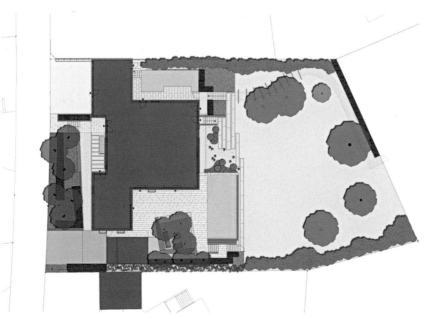

Site plan

This garden's professional design created a unique oasis, completely adapted to the desires, needs and uses that were stipulated by the owners.

STILL

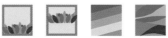

YOTSUKAIDO CITY, CHIBA PREF., JAPAN

Architect // **Satoshi Kurosaki | APOLLO Architects & Associates**
Photographer // © **Masao Nishikawa**

The introverted layout of this two-story, reinforced concrete house responds to the occupants' search for a peaceful retreat and their need for privacy. The building is set back from a street with heavy traffic. Other than a narrow entry hall and a garage facing this street, the house has few exterior windows. On the other hand, the massive concrete walls conceal open spaces with floor to ceiling glass partitions that open to light-filled courtyards and balconies. Both floors look into a central courtyard with a mature maple and an open riser stair. Once inside the house, the peaceful atmosphere sets the mood for relaxation and contemplation, away from the tumultuous environment outside the concrete walls.

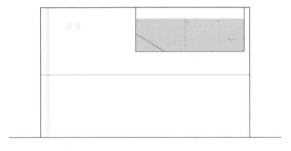

North elevation

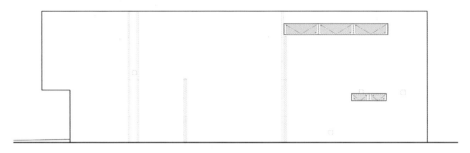

East elevation

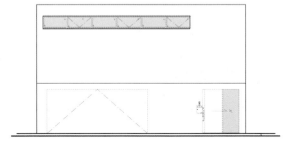

South elevation

West elevation

This house, made of concrete, steel, and glass, adds to the geometry of its design. At the same time, it is a neutral background for the greenery of its various courtyards.

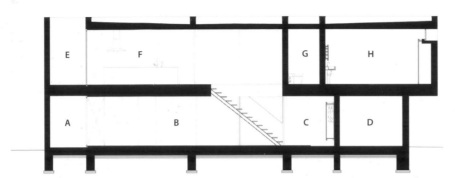

A. Terrace
B. Hallway
C. Entry hall
D. Bicycle parking
E. Balcony
F. Living/Dining/Kitchen
G. Bathroom/WC
H. Child's room
I. Garage
J. Bedroom
K. Playroom
L. Pantry
M. Walk-in closet

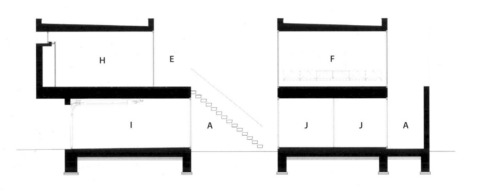

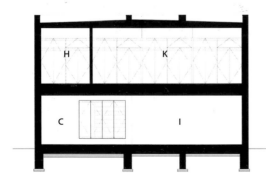

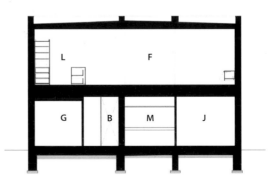

Sections

The architects maximize the connection between interior and exterior spaces by means of bridges, balconies, and glassed-in corridors around a central courtyard that gives the house a Zen atmosphere.

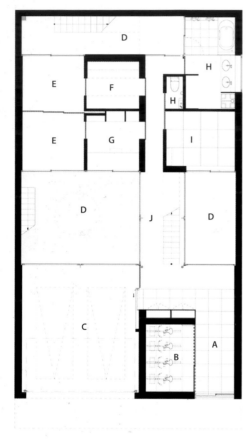

Ground floor plan

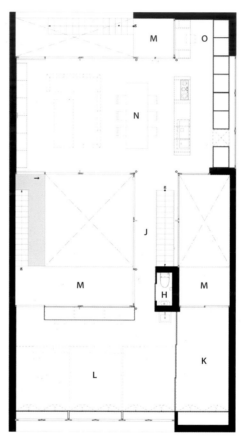

Second floor plan

A. Entry hall
B. Bicycle parking
C. Garage
D. Terrace
E. Bedroom
F. Walk-in closet
G. Study
H. Bathroom/WC
I. Guestroom
J. Hallway
K. Child`s room
L. Playroom
M. Balcony
N. Living/
   Dining/Kitchen
O. Pantry

The introverted layout of the house is in response to the client's request for a house where he could find peace and silence. The central courtyard can be enjoyed from the two levels of the house.

THE UNLIKELY
TWINS

COLOMBES, FRANCE

Architect // **Barthélemy-Ifrah Architecture**

Photographers // © Yves Marchand and Romain Meffre

The site of a disused car garage is the starting point for a challenging residential project. The programmatic differences between the existing conditions and the new construction led to the demolition of almost the entire structure. Making the most of the available space with a tight budget and creating a structure that allowed as much light in as possible were the main driving motives of the house design. The light issue was resolved with the creation of an inner patio delimited by glass enclosures, while the layout of the house articulates the various public and private domains in a number of spatial turns that heighten spatial experience.

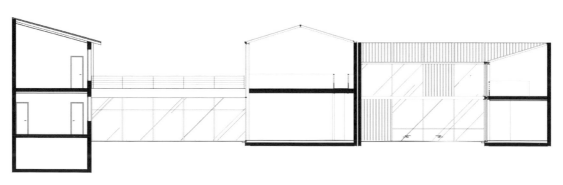

Section

Ground floor plan

Second floor plan

A fully glazed patio is the starting point for this project. The house, wedged between a police station and a dense urban landscape, needs to be flooded with light.

CABO HOUSE

BENAVIDEZ, BUENOS AIRES, ARGENTINA

Architect // **Andrés Remy Arquitectos**
Landscape architect // **Leandro La Bella**
Photographer // © **Alejandro Peral**

This contemporary house is the new home for an elderly couple who wanted to move out from their too large family house to a much smaller and functional dwelling. The design is compact with two sides facing a lake. The south-oriented front side is solid, preserving the occupant's privacy. The north and east sides open up toward the lake and the best views. The minimalist design of the house is reflected in the simple but striking landscape design, which is carried out into the interior of the house. An interior patio, with plants and wood platforms that echo the "stepping stones" at the front of the house, minimizes the boundaries between exterior and interior spaces.

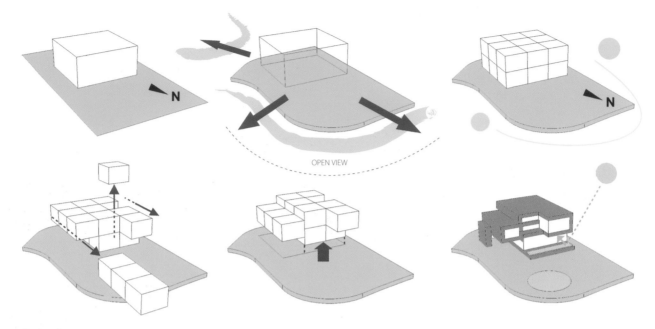

Massing diagrams

PUBLIC

PRIVATE

SERVICE

GREEN SPACES

CIRCULATION

WATER

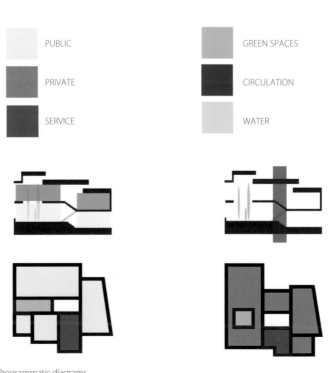

Programmatic diagrams

The pool is strategically located on the edge of the plot, where it enjoys all-day sun and benefits from the best views of the lake.

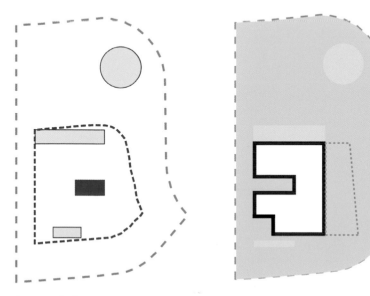

Programmatic diagrams

A. Hall
B. Patio
C. Living room
D. Dining room
E. Kitchen
F. Guest bathroom
G. Outdoor dining
H. Garage
I. Staff bedroom
J. Reflective pool
K. Pool
L. Garden
M. Master bedroom
N. Master bathroom
O. Balcony
P. Office
Q. Bedroom
R. Bathroom
S. Laundry room
T. Storage

Second floor plan

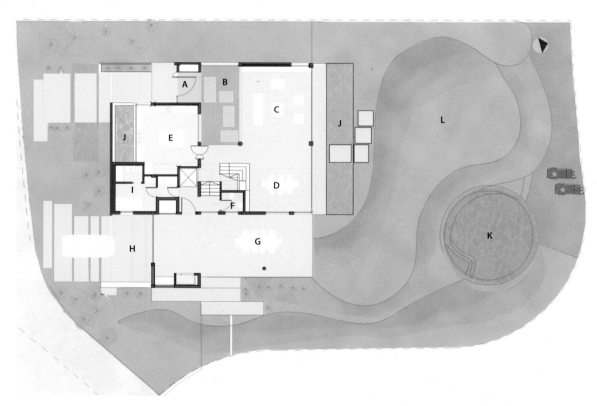

Ground floor plan

Inside, a double-height central green space allows the air to circulate freely, provides indirect overhead lighting, and crisscrosses the views from one area of the house to another.

GUESTHOUSE

AUSTIN, TX, USA

Architects // **Miró Rivera Architects**

Photographer // © Paul Finkel | Piston Design

Located on a two-acre peninsula, this guesthouse is accessed from the main house via a pedestrian bridge made of steel rebar left unfinished to rust and merge with the surrounding landscape. The guesthouse is surrounded by reed-filled wetlands that serve as a migratory stop for egrets, cranes, and swans. Hence, its design responds to a meticulous analysis of the surrounding vegetation and wildlife to implement a ten-year plan that will restore and expand the area of the existing wetlands, eliminate invasive plants, and reintroduce native species. With a small footprint to minimize environmental impact, the house can remind one of a bird-watching tower, encouraging interaction with the natural environment.

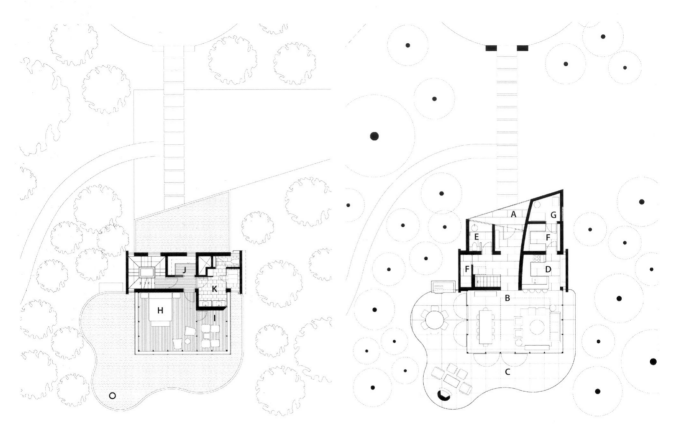

Ground floor plan

Second floor plan

A. Entry
B. Dining/Living area
C. Terrace
D. Kitchen
E. Powder room
F. Storage

G. Mechanical room
H. Bedroom
I. Balcony
J. Closet
K. Bathroom

The beauty of the natural landscape informs many aspects of the project. Access to the guesthouse is via a pedestrian bridge inspired by the reeds surrounding the site.

A glass box above the first floor roof has shutters that can accommodate varying light conditions. The windows are fully operable, encouraging greater interaction with the surroundings.

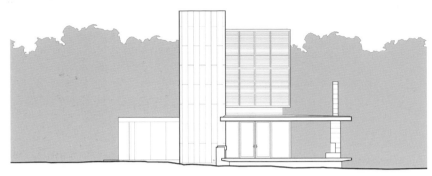

West elevation

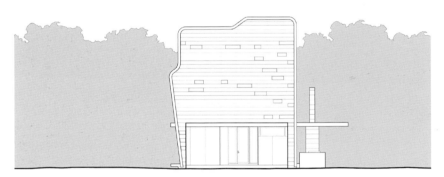

North elevation

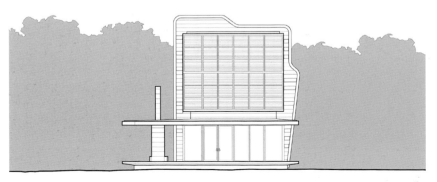

East elevation

The ground floor is completely open to the surrounding terrace, separated only by floor-to-ceiling glass. The sweeping covered deck appears to float above the ground.

REFORMA
HOUSE

LOMAS DE CHAPULTEPEC, MEXICO

Architect // **Central de Arquitectura**

Photographer // © **Central de Arquitectura**

Clarity, simplicity, and honesty are the defining qualities of this house. A minimal palette of materials and colors emphasizes the strong geometric interplay of vertical and horizontal planes that form the house and its harmonic balance between solid and void. Various water features mirror the composition, giving the illusion that the house is floating and enhancing its dynamic character. The open plan of the house and large spans of glass offer unrestricted views beyond the stone walls of the property, while its dimensions make it an opulent retreat perfectly suitable for entertaining. Terraces and decks contribute to the modern day indoor-outdoor lifestyle.

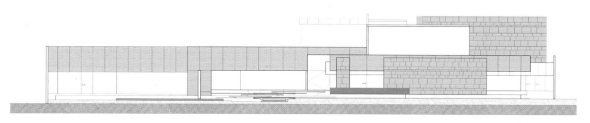

Main elevation

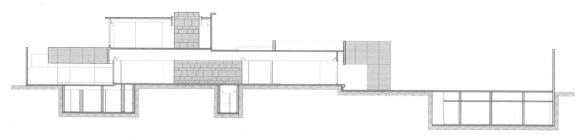

Longitudinal section

The design was inspired by the geometries of the urban context. This led to the creation of solid stone volumes, which also responded to the horizontality and the proportions generated by the spaces.

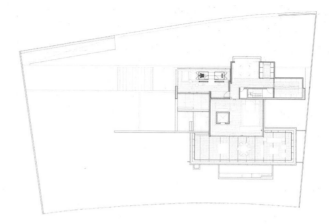

Second floor plan

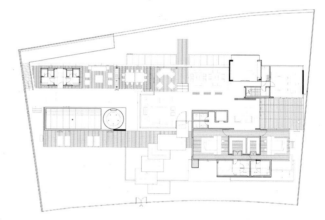

Ground floor plan

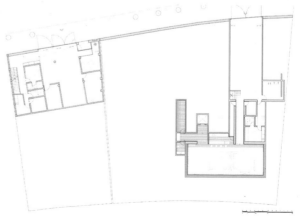

Basement floor plan

The interior spaces are free of obstructions that could interrupt the dialogue between the interior and the exterior. They effortlessly spill onto the pool and shaded outdoor dining area.

STEIN HOUSE

ORINDA, CA, USA

Architect // **Swatt | Miers Architects**
Landscape architect // **Thuilot Associates**
Photographer // © **Russell Abraham**

On a majestic ridge with sweeping views of hillsides and valleys, Stein House is a makeover of an original single-story, tile-roof ranch house. Although the house was advantageously located on the southwest part of the property, it suffered from low ceilings, a disjointed floor plan, and minimal glazing that failed to address the beautiful views. The makeover, which is limited to the footprint of the existing building, optimizes the connection between the house and the landscape. In this respect, deep overhangs allow interior spaces to spill onto the exterior, while fragmenting the long and narrow proportions of the house in a rhythmic composition further enhanced by the use of materials.

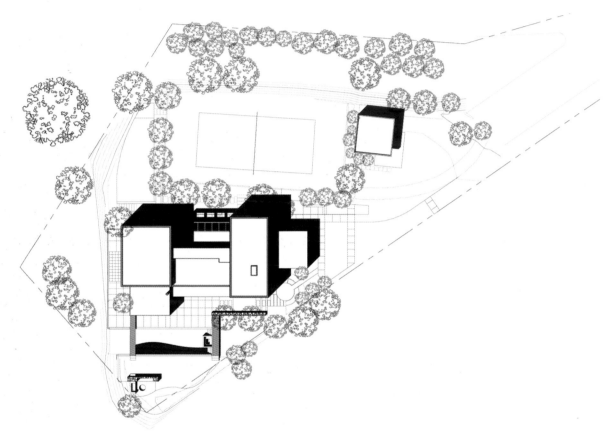

Site plan

When this old ranch house was renovated, water took on a pivotal role: a series of small ponds on the outer perimeter of the home gives it a new personality.

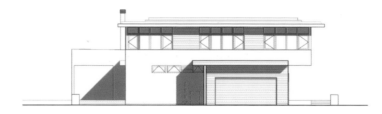

East elevation

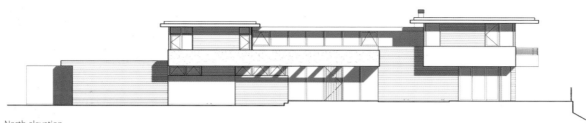

North elevation

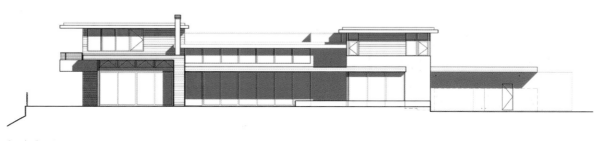

South elevation

West elevation

The large windows, balconies, and pool deck work together to provide spectacular panoramic views of the valley and surrounding hills.

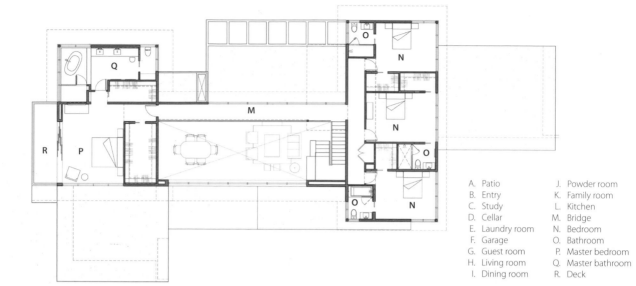

A. Patio
B. Entry
C. Study
D. Cellar
E. Laundry room
F. Garage
G. Guest room
H. Living room
I. Dining room
J. Powder room
K. Family room
L. Kitchen
M. Bridge
N. Bedroom
O. Bathroom
P. Master bedroom
Q. Master bathroom
R. Deck

Second floor plan

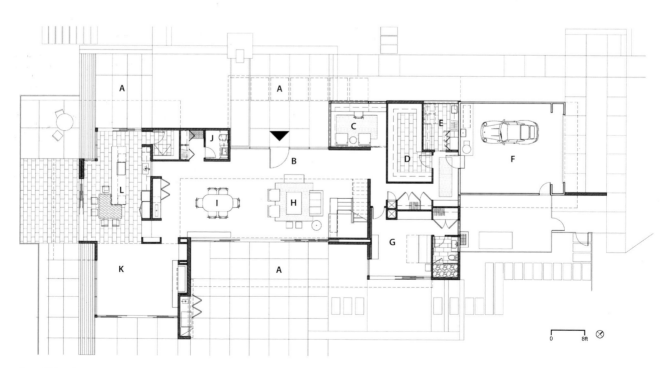

Ground floor plan

OZ RESIDENCE

SILICON VALLEY, CA, USA

Architect // **Swatt | Miers Architects**
Landscape architect // **Ron Herman Landscape Architect**
Photographer // © **Tim Griffith**

The owners, a couple with three young children, wanted their home to have a casual, barefoot feel, like a vacation destination. Their almost three-acre site, with gentle slopes to the south and mature landscaping on all sides, was the perfect setting to create a home that would fully engage the beautiful landscape. The 10,000-square-foot home is organized into an L-shaped plan with two wings joined at a two-story great room. Sheathed in mahogany boards and fully glazed on two sides, this beautiful volume is pierced by a floating glass bridge that both connects and separates the family and sleeping wings on either side.

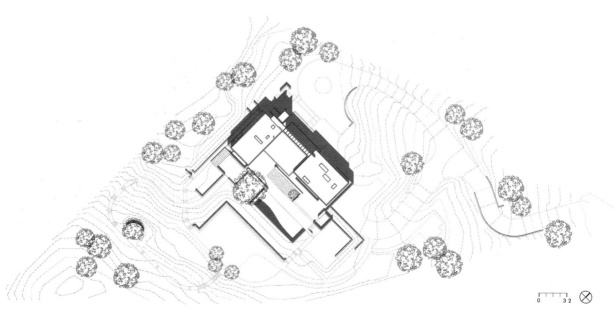

Site plan

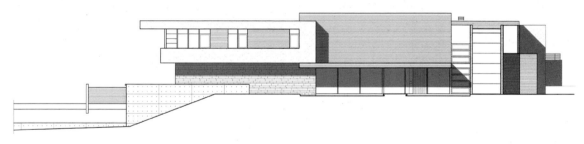

North elevation

East elevation

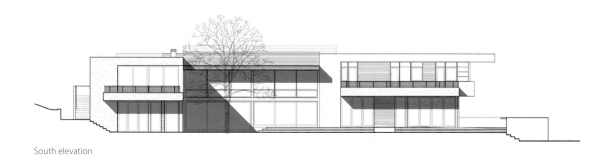

South elevation

West elevation

This property combines large glazed areas with natural mahogany wood cladding on the facade. This same type of wood is used to cover the entire area around the swimming pool.

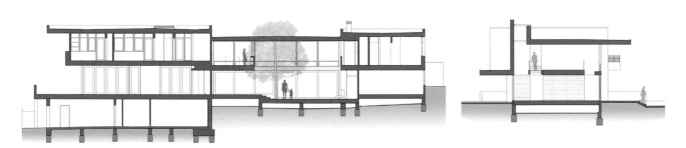

Sections

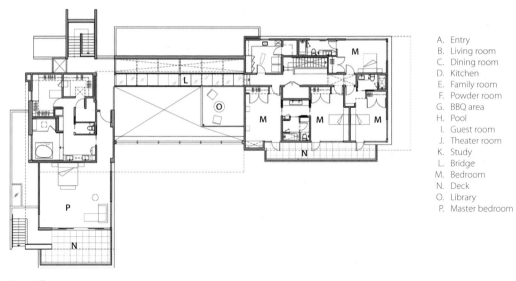

A. Entry
B. Living room
C. Dining room
D. Kitchen
E. Family room
F. Powder room
G. BBQ area
H. Pool
I. Guest room
J. Theater room
K. Study
L. Bridge
M. Bedroom
N. Deck
O. Library
P. Master bedroom

Second floor plan

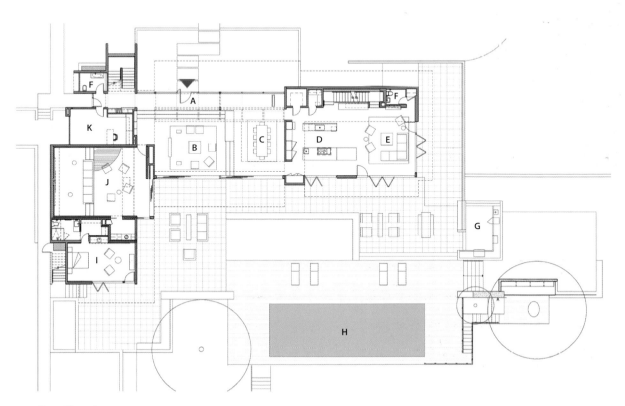

Ground floor plan

MANDEVILLE CANYON

LOS ANGELES, CA, USA

Architect // **Griffin Enright Architects**

Photographer // © **Tim Street-Porter**

This project is sited on a cul-de-sac that creates a tapered lot with a small front yard contrasting with an expansive backyard with city views. The house becomes an overscaled porch with a discrete entrance and deliberate entry sequence that reveals the views. From the backyard, the house is seen as horizontal layers that seem to emerge from the landscape, while the sensation at the entrance of the house is distinctly more urban and vertical. The walls fold into roof surfaces, anchoring the horizontal qualities of the terrain. The living room level is subtly lifted from the ground, creating a layer of terracing that extends the topographic shifts of the landscape into the house.

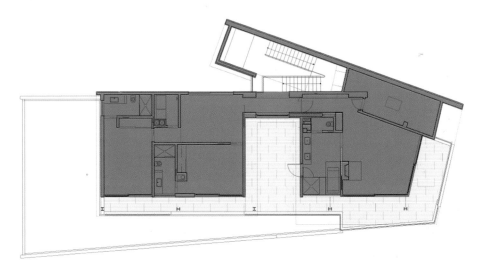

Second floor plan

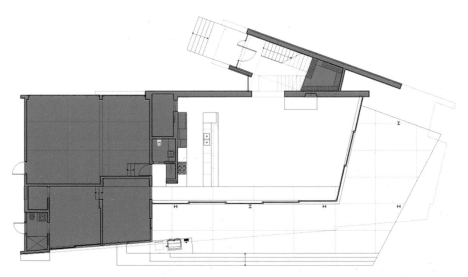

First floor plan

The dichotomy between the understated street presence and the openness of the backyard enhances the experience of discovering the sweeping views upon entering the house.

The second floor slab serves as a plinth for the master bedroom and children's bedrooms, which are separated by an open court. This split configuration contrasts with the continuity of the lower floor.

The open glazed facades with large porches protect the interior spaces from harsh sunlight in the summer and allow winter light to extend into the house for passive heating.

MILL VALLEY
HOUSE

MILL VALLEY, CA, USA

Architect // **CCS Architecture**

Photographer // © **Paul Dyer**

Given the specifics of the house location, stepping up the hillside and squeezed between red-woods, the home is divided into three levels. The lower floor is partially built into the hillside, while the upper two levels enjoy abundant daylight and views. Exposed concrete and copper cladding were used as materials that will change over time, evolving toward a greater integration with the surrounding natural landscape. The interior has a gallery feel. Its large windows frame the views of the redwood grove and the valley below the house, almost like art on the walls.

Intimate connections to groves of redwood trees and the steepness of the site are the inspiration, and the guiding element, for the architecture of this house.

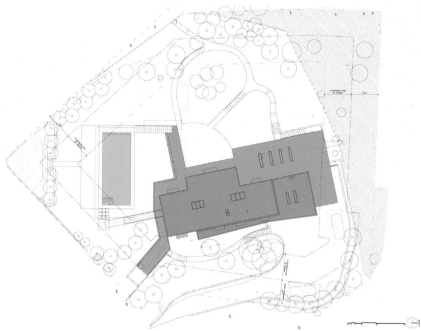

Site plan

Second floor plan

Ground floor plan

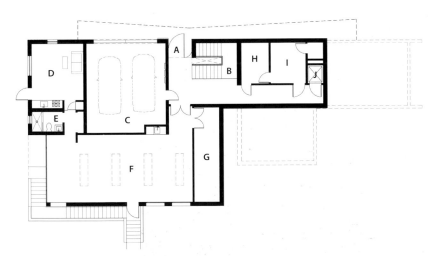

Basement floor plan

A. Entry
B. Stair to main living level
C. Garage
D. Guest quarters
E. Bathroom
F. Painting studio
G. Painting storage
H. Storage
I. Boiler/Hot water heater
J. Elevator
K. Stairs from below
L. Living room
M. Kitchen
N. Desk
O. Pantry
P. Dining room
Q. Stair to second floor
R. Powder room
S. Laundry room
T. Deck
U. Master bedroom
V. Master bathroom
W. Dressing room
X. Guest room
Y. Office
Z. Ramp to yard and pool

The main living level connects to the outdoors as much as possible through glass sliding doors, leading to a deck only a few feet away from a grove of ancient redwoods.

WESTRIDGE RESIDENCE

LOS ANGELES, CA, USA

Architect // **Montalba Architects**

Landscape architect // **Venice Studio, Polly Furr**

Photographer // © **John Linden**

A dark single-story construction is transformed into a light-filled home, making the most of its spectacular hilltop location with some of the best views in the area. The new design included the renovation of the existing structure and the addition of a second floor to satisfy the spatial requirements. The owners needed a home where they could entertain and host a large extended family, where guests would feel at home during prolonged visits. To accommodate this need, the architects designed a plan with a central communal space on the lower floor, three private zones around, it and a fourth private zone on the second floor as part of the extension.

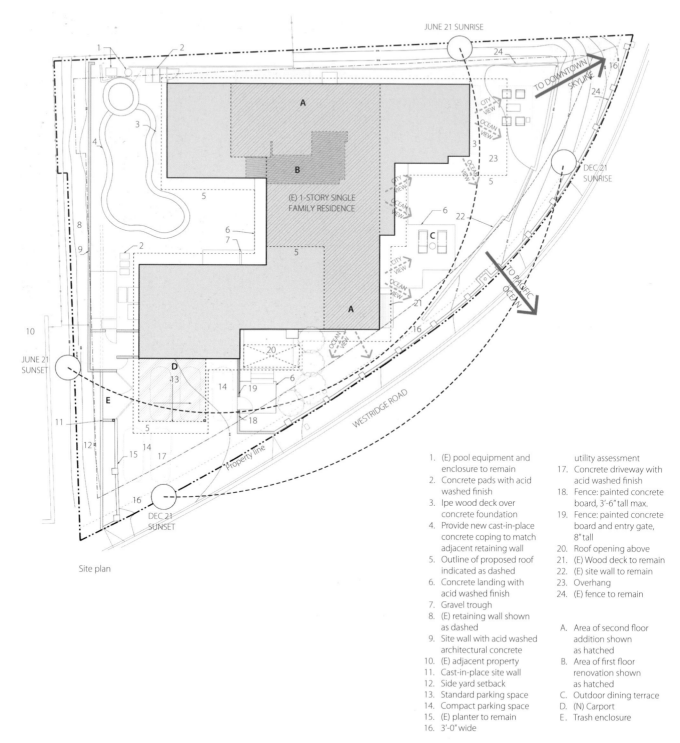

JUNE 21 SUNRISE

TO DOWNTOWN SKYLINE

DEC 21 SUNRISE

(E) 1-STORY SINGLE FAMILY RESIDENCE

TO PACIFIC OCEAN

CITY VIEW
OCEAN VIEW

JUNE 21 SUNSET

DEC 21 SUNSET

WESTRIDGE ROAD

Property line

Site plan

1. (E) pool equipment and enclosure to remain
2. Concrete pads with acid washed finish
3. Ipe wood deck over concrete foundation
4. Provide new cast-in-place concrete coping to match adjacent retaining wall
5. Outline of proposed roof indicated as dashed
6. Concrete landing with acid washed finish
7. Gravel trough
8. (E) retaining wall shown as dashed
9. Site wall with acid washed architectural concrete
10. (E) adjacent property
11. Cast-in-place site wall
12. Side yard setback
13. Standard parking space
14. Compact parking space
15. (E) planter to remain
16. 3'-0" wide

17. Concrete driveway with acid washed finish
18. Fence: painted concrete board, 3'-6" tall max.
19. Fence: painted concrete board and entry gate, 8" tall
20. Roof opening above
21. (E) Wood deck to remain
22. (E) site wall to remain
23. Overhang
24. (E) fence to remain

A. Area of second floor addition shown as hatched
B. Area of first floor renovation shown as hatched
C. Outdoor dining terrace
D. (N) Carport
E. Trash enclosure

utility assessment

Floor plan

In the remodeling and expansion of the second floor, the architects transformed the roofs to frame views of downtown Los Angeles and the Pacific Ocean with an innovative approach using horizontal decks.

The clean lines, connection between exterior and interior, palette, gentle breeze, and sea views create the effect of a contemporary beach house, despite its location on a hill.

PORTIO GARDEN

PLAYA DE PORTIO, CANTABRIA, SPAIN

Landscape architect // **David Añíbarro Paisajismo**

Photographer // © **David Añíbarro**

The contemporary design of a house and its location in a coastal environment with high levels of salinity were the conditioning factors that dictated the design of this garden. On the one hand, wind-resistant plant varieties were selected in response to the often rough climate conditions of the area. On the other hand, a clear geometry created a compartmentalized garden, in which different spaces are connected through a unifying feature: a silica gravel path. An L-shaped planting bed is the origin of the garden design. The lines of its sides are offset and extended to create a grid that generates the path, the landscaped areas with different plant combinations, the lawn, an outdoor dining area, and a small pond.

Garden plan. Volume and color study.

Extending from the terrace and pool, an L-shaped planter is the starting point from which all of the house's exterior design lines begin. It also increases the size of the terrace in the garden.

The subdivision of the garden results in a series of spaces that occur along the length of the gravel path, creating a type of corridor that leads you between the different areas of vegetation.

Δ Texturas / vd superficie

Planting sketch

APARICIO GARDEN

NAVAJEDA, CANTABRIA, SPAIN

Landscape architect // **David Añíbarro Paisajismo**
Photographer // © **David Añíbarro**

This garden was designed for one of a series of row houses with low retaining walls between them that offer no privacy. To resolve this situation, the design of this garden focused on lining the walls with plantings of different heights and textures that provide a natural feel. Then, a pattern of arcs on the ground plane was created to soften the angular perimeter of the property and to reinforce the natural effect. The arcs acquire greater significance when they are understood as the means to articulate the different areas of the garden, taking into account the views from the house, its various entry points, and the exterior circulation.

Based on a series of arcs that follow the perimeter of the garden, this design provides a solution
to the home's exits, views, and general move-
ment between the different rooms.

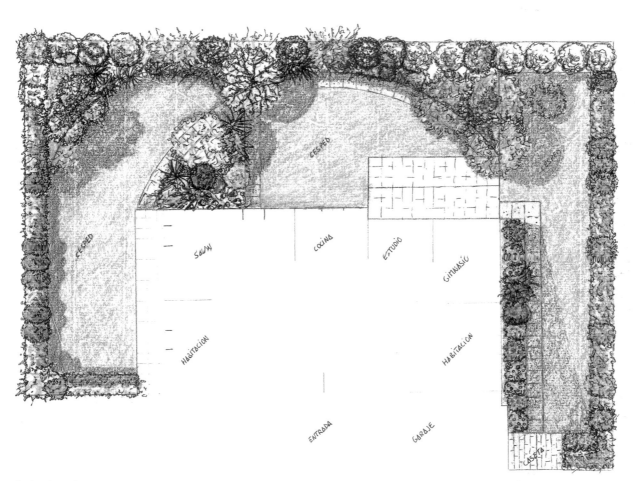

Garden plan. Volume and color study.

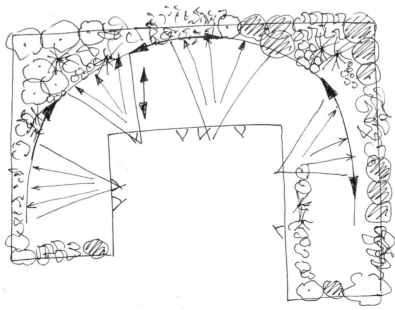

Planting sketches

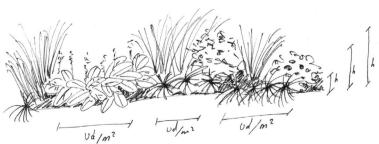

Planting sketches

The diverse shapes and shades of green plant varieties, together with their staggered blooms, help to create an environment that changes with the seasons, giving a richness to the house's surroundings.

Planting sketches

DWELLING
AND FICUS

SAN ANTONIO DE ESCAZÚ, COSTA RICA

Architect // **Cañas Arquitectos**

Photographer // © **Ricardo Chaves**

"The ficus was already there when the house was built. The house came to coexist with the ficus and give prominence to the site. Both are now an indissoluble whole." (Cañas Arquitectos). The program could not be simpler: a place to enjoy the scenery and the company of family and friends. The site has a slight slope toward the east, offering spectacular views of the city of San José with the Escazú mountain range as a backdrop. The house, with three glass sides and a sloped roof, opens up toward the views, while a wooden deck on steel posts strengthens the connection between the house and the natural surroundings. In short, a transparent and lightweight house designed to be genuinely immersed in the landscape.

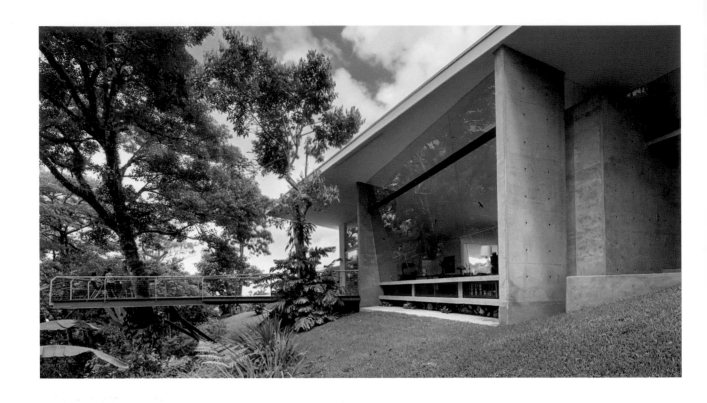

Site plan

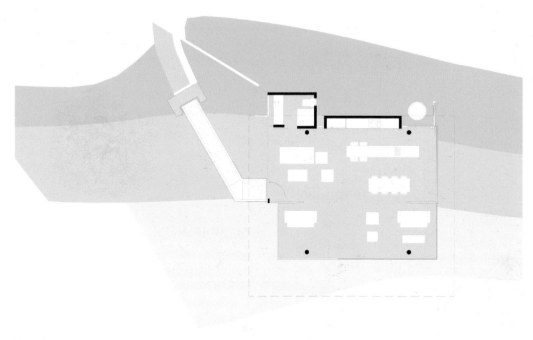

Floor plan

The design takes in a huge fig tree, incorporating it in the large terrace and, at dusk, letting it compete with the lights that rise from the nearby city of San José.

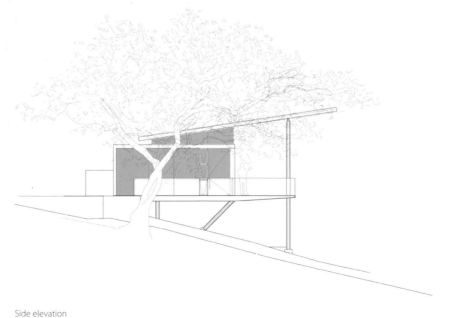

Side elevation

GINGKO PROJECT

BEEKBERGEN, THE NETHERLANDS

Architect // **Casanova+Hernandez Architects**

Photographer // © **Christian Richters**

The "Ginkgo" project is a housing complex that is physically and visually integrated in its context. The site is an interesting space located between two zones with very different characters: a green park on one side and an urban, postwar neighborhood built in the 1950s on the other side. The most striking feature of the building is its glazed facade, which features a print of *Ginkgo Biloba* tree leaves that reacts to the constant changing light, creating reflections, shadows, and silhouettes. This innovative treatment of the building skin provides privacy along the balconies and terraces, while ensuring visual connection between the outdoor spaces and the park.

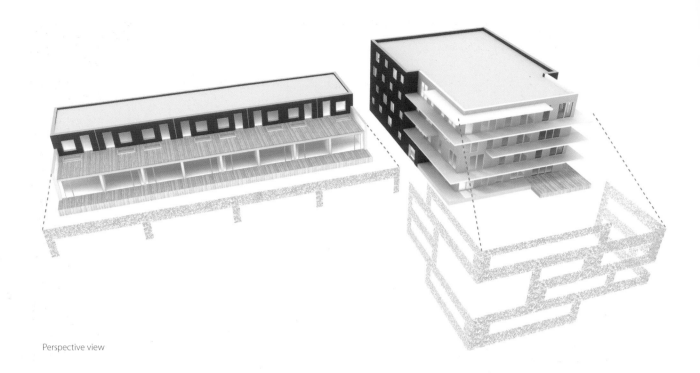

Perspective view

The Ginkgo project seeks to combine art, technology, and architecture with the aim of integrating every one of its homes in the natural environment of the park where it is located.

The building is compact, with minimum surface area and maximum isolation. The balconies along the south and west facades provide natural protection from the sun during the summer.

Elevation

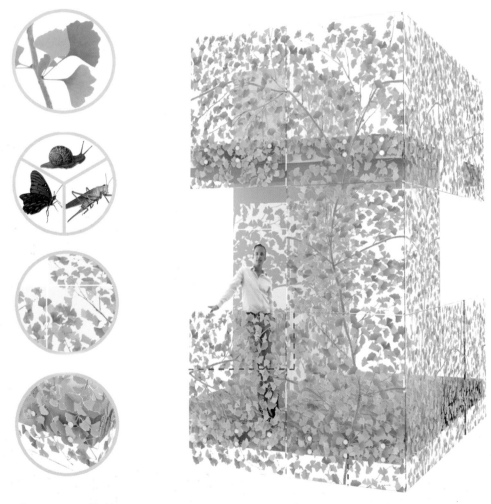

3D representation of building corner

Partial block second floor plan

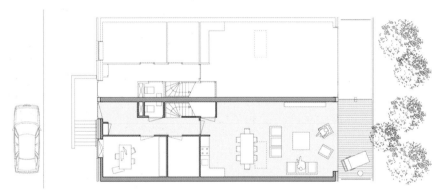

Partial block ground floor plan

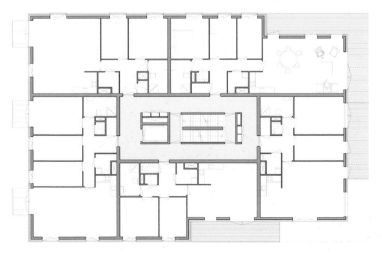

Standard block floor plan

There is a dialogue between two "skins": the green skin that connects with the park, evident in the transparency of the facade, and the urban skin, which connects with the adjacent buildings through the use of brick.

URBAN ROOF GARDEN

MADRID, SPAIN

Landscape architect // **La Habitación Verde**

Photographer // © **La Habitación Verde**

This project proposes the optimization of a reduced outdoor space by means of a built-in wooden element that adapts to different roles: bench, daybed, trunk, and planter. This solution resolves myriad situations, while freeing up space for other uses such as dining and lounging. The terrace opens the apartment to the views of the city. It enables social and private uses by simply changing the configuration of the wooden element. The terrace also fulfills the functions of an outdoor living area, while serving as a green backdrop for the interior living space.

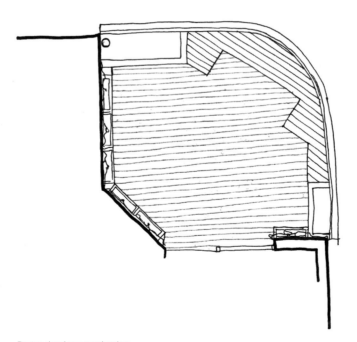

Design development sketches

There were two key objectives in the design of this penthouse's exterior spaces: to open the terrace to the stunning views and to increase the living area by optimizing the available space.

Design development sketches

Plants screen and direct the views: a backdrop of bamboo obscures the city views to the side, while the alignment of small, aromatic herbs in the planter to the front allows you to enjoy the views.

BEACH HOUSE
ON A HILL

LIMA, PERU

Architect // **Artadi Architects**

Photographers // © **Alfio Garozzo, Elsa Ramírez**

The steepness of the site was a challenge creatively met by the architect. Wedged between two parallel retaining walls, the house is cut into the hillside, maximizing views from every level. It sits on top of a pedestal containing the private domain of the dwelling. Two cantilevering floor slabs counterbalance the verticality of the retaining wall. The top one is the roof, which also serves as a driveway and as terrace with unobstructed views. The floor below is the second slab, which accommodates a spacious living area and a pool. Positioned at the top of a hill, the house is a lookout offering views of the valley below and the sea beyond.

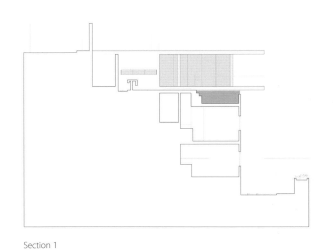

Section 1

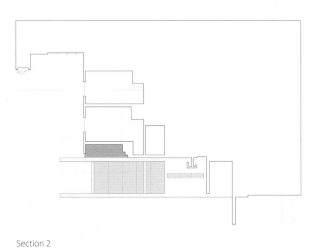

Section 2

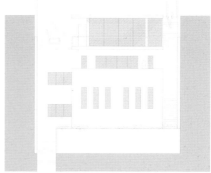

Southeast elevation

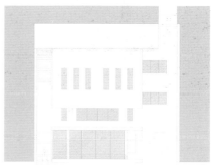

Northwest elevation

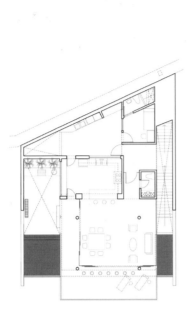

Third floor plan

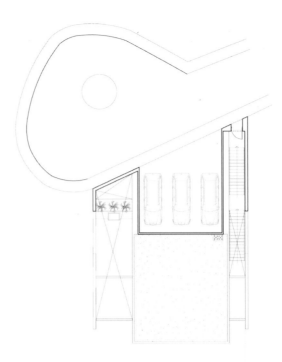

Fourth floor plan

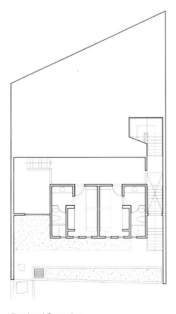

First level floor plan

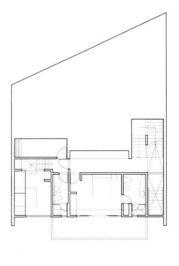

Second floor plan

Situated on a high pedestal, two large parallel planes host a large social area, which appears to lose gravity, flying into the void and floating on the water of the pool.

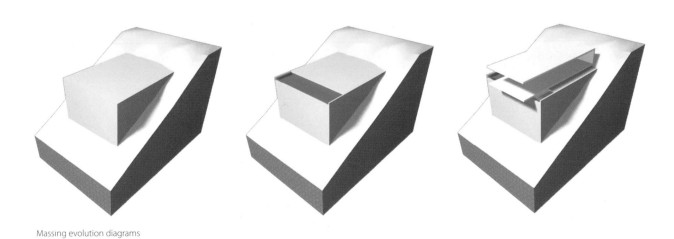

Massing evolution diagrams

GARDEN HOUSE

LA ESTADÍA, MEXICO

Architect // Jorge Hernández de la Garza

Photographer // © Jorge Hernández de la Garza

The house responds to the topography of the site, allotting the architectural program in three staked rectangular volumes. These volumes are wrapped in a continuous plane, anchoring the house to the natural slope of the terrain. Furthermore, this plane generates a series of overhangs to protect the various outdoor areas on all three levels. The encompassing landscape motivated the architects to design habitable green roofs that merge with the scenery. They are used for outdoor activities, especially during the summer months. In this respect, the living and dining areas morph and connect with the outside by means of a terrace that appears to float above the rest of the construction.

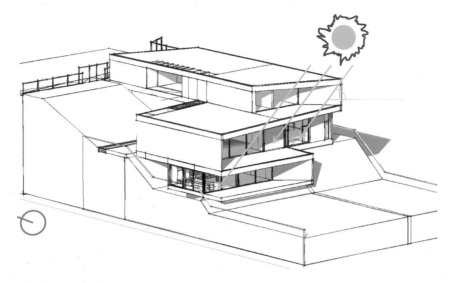

Beneficial use of sunlight in winter

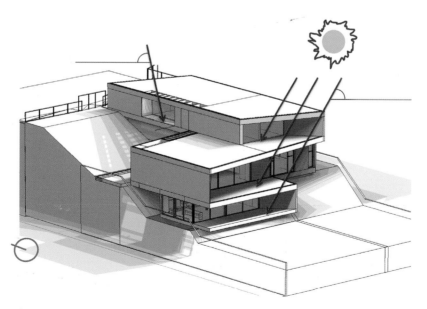

Sun protection in spring and summer

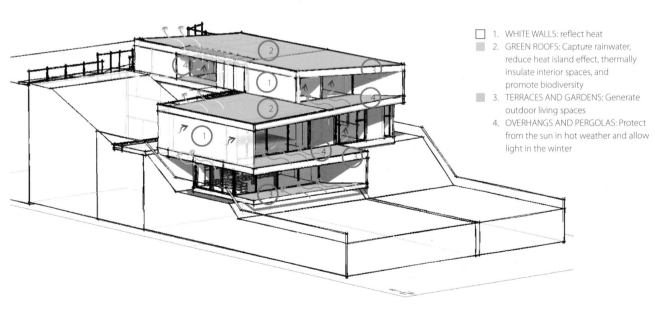

Bioclimatic strategy diagram

1. WHITE WALLS: reflect heat
2. GREEN ROOFS: Capture rainwater, reduce heat island effect, thermally insulate interior spaces, and promote biodiversity
3. TERRACES AND GARDENS: Generate outdoor living spaces
4. OVERHANGS AND PERGOLAS: Protect from the sun in hot weather and allow light in the winter

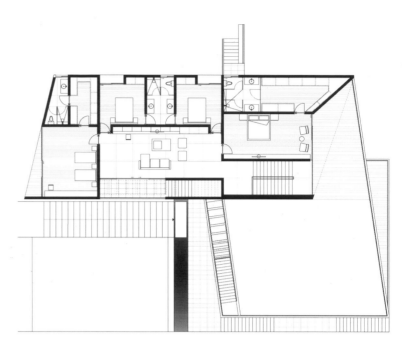

Top level floor plan

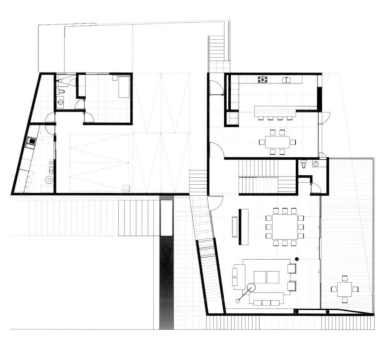

Lower floor plan

Midlevel floor plan

The symbiosis between this house and its natural environment is unique: green roofs promote a biodiversity of insects that, in turn and over time, increases plant diversity in the area.

AB
FABUL'HOUSE

SURESNES, FRANCE

Architect // **Barthélemy-Ifrah Architecture**

Photographers // © Yves Marchand and Romain Meffre

The land on which this house is built is interesting in more than one way. The area is generous, but it also has the added advantage of being covered with a dense vegetation which led the architects to conceive a design that harmonizes with nature. The strong relationship between nature and construction is manifested by a strip of vegetation that serves as organizer of the house interior. Access to the house is through the lower floor, which, despite being partially underground, comes out onto the largest open area of the property. The living area is naturally on the upper floor, taking full advantage of large expanses of glass that let in abundant light and give access to a terrace.

The dense vegetation on this land led to the creation of a project that would take nature into account: a large, planted strip divides the house into two parts, providing light and entangling the house in the ground.

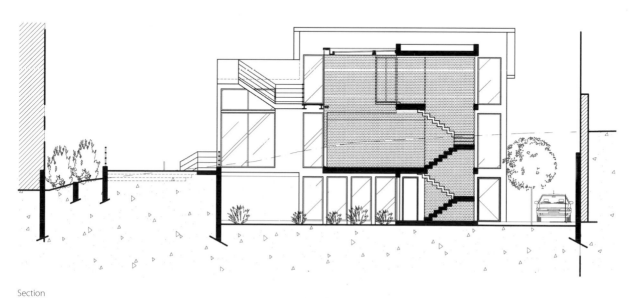

Section

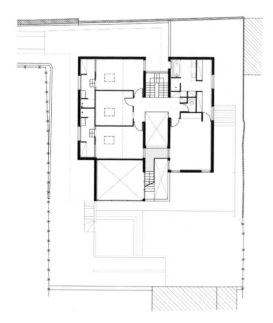

Upper floor plan

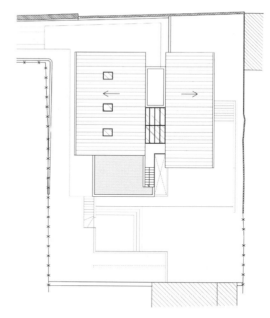

Roof plan

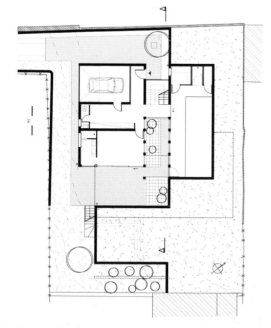

Basement floor plan

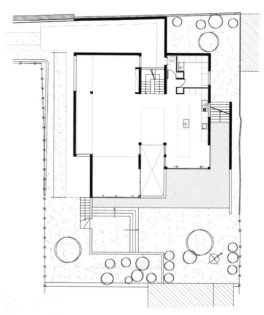

Ground floor plan

257

ACASSUSO HOUSE

ACASSUSO, BUENOS AIRES, ARGENTINA

Architect // **Andrés Remy Arquitectos**

Photographer // © **Andrés Remy Arquitectos**

It's hard to perceive just how densely developed this site is. Although the floor area of this single-family house exceeds the area of the site, it seems as if it's a house set in an ample garden, shaded by trees. The architects pulled off this trick by tucking much of the volume of the house under a series of richly landscaped and flooded roof terraces. They then punctured the house through with a deep courtyard, light wells, and a breezeway, which connects the deep well of the courtyard to the open backyard. These punctures set up an intricate series of spaces, interlacing the exterior with the interior and allowing every habitable room to open onto the garden through wide glass openings.

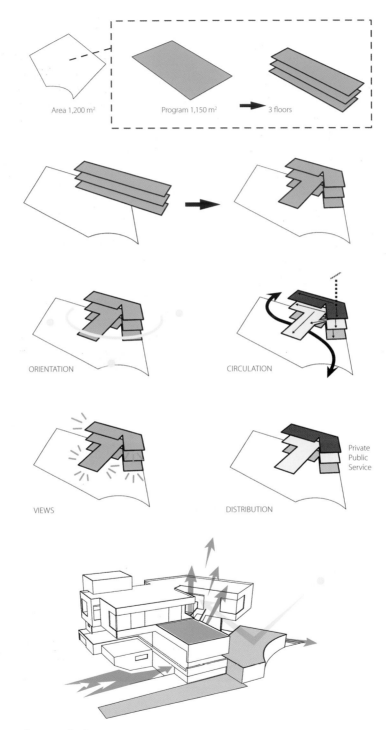

Area 1,200 m²

Program 1,150 m²

3 floors

ORIENTATION

CIRCULATION

VIEWS

DISTRIBUTION

Private
Public
Service

Programmatic diagrams

Perspective view

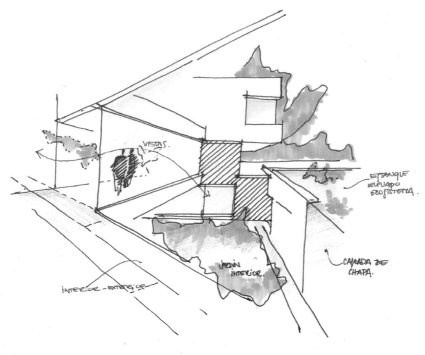

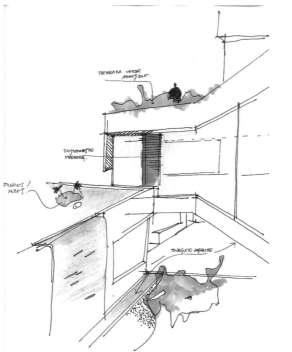

Perspective views

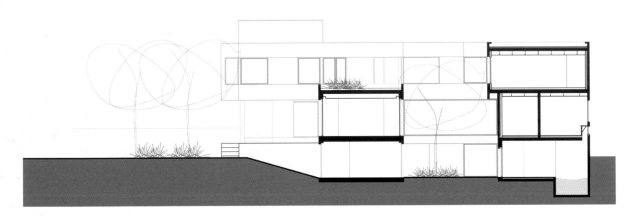

Section A-A

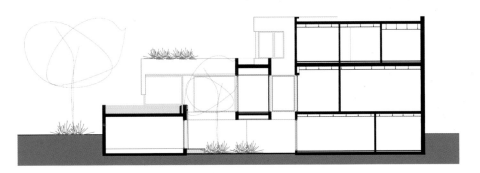

Section B-B

A large pond initiates the flow of water, which pours over another pond in an inner courtyard. The house appears to be shaped by the stream like a hill: the green platforms are the result of erosion that never happened.

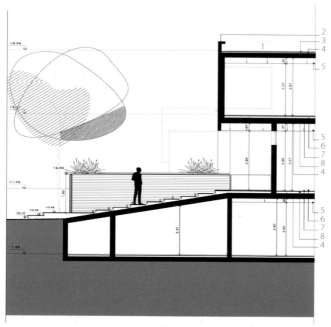

Detailed partial section

1. Accessible rooftop
2. Exposed concrete
3. Slope 2%
4. Reinforced concrete slab
5. Durlock® dropped ceiling
6. Finish 3 cm
7. Subfloor
8. Radiant floor 8 cm

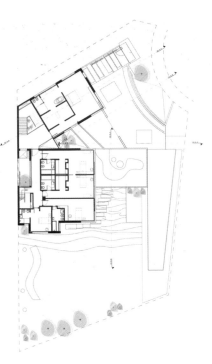

Second floor plan

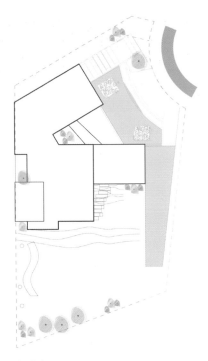

Roof plan

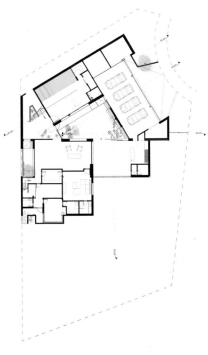

Basement floor plan

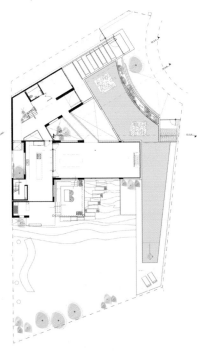

Ground floor plan

The house penetrates the ground via the inner courtyards. "A landscape made into a home," as the architects say, but not just any landscape. The house beautifully integrates its surroundings to create a seamless indoor/outdoor environment.

Andrés Remy is a champion of sustainable architecture using natural resources. "The important thing is to consider the location," he claims. A river runs nearby, so the house owes much to the water.

SKY GARDEN HOUSE

SENTOSA ISLAND, SINGAPORE

Architect // **Guz Architects**

Photographer // © Patrick Bingham-Hall

Sky Garden, a ziggurat-shaped tropical hanging garden, sits aside the storied Singapore Strait. A thick planting bed is provided at each roof level, forming a terraced garden for the level above. Wide eaves stretch far out, providing deep shade below and larger garden terrace areas above. The highest level is capped with an arched roof, like the apex of a grassy knoll. Two typical tropical materials, white stucco and natural wood planks, form the built backdrop for the verdant growth that is everywhere. And rising up through the center is a single tall open-air space around which the house is organized.

The green roofs on each floor are edged with louver canopies that extend over the floor immediately below to provide shade.

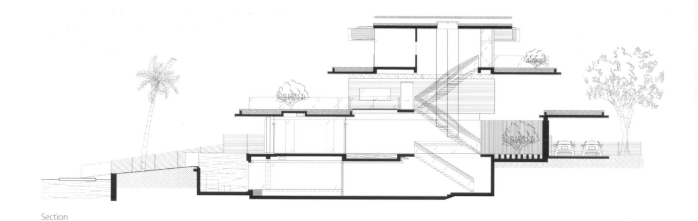

Section

The building is terraced, allowing each story to have visual and physical connection with a landscaped area. This creates a layered effect that reduces the scale of the building.

An inner courtyard on the garage level provides the two lower floors with light and ventilation. Conceptually, it "anchors" the house to the site and makes for an impressive entry.

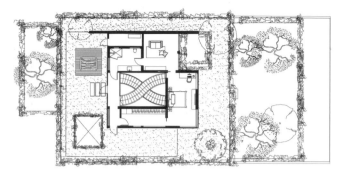

Third floor plan

Second floor plan

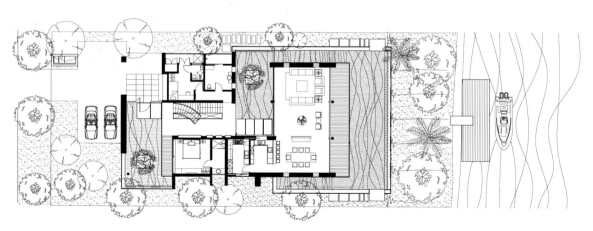

Ground floor plan

VG RESIDENCE

LOS ANGELES, CA, USA

Architect // **Eric Rosen Architects**
Photographer // © **Erich Koyama**

This house perches above the Pacific, atop a dramatic rocky outcrop. A grassy courtyard bound by the house on three sides and open across a pool to sweeping views on the fourth side comprises a large outdoor "room" that organizes the house. Paralleling each interior room is a well-formed exterior space: an entry court that caps the long passage to the house along the site's panhandle from the street, a patio at the extreme reach of the living room wing with the most exposure possible to the panoramic views, and a sheltered and shaded terrace just outside the dinning room. This variety of exterior rooms is capped off by a suite of rooftop spaces that are situated to even better capture this site's breathtaking vistas.

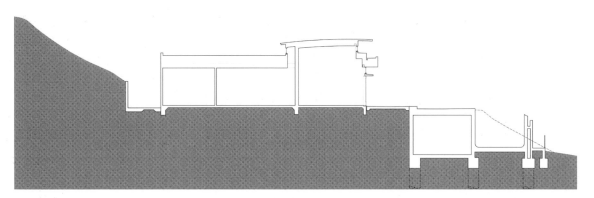

Section AA

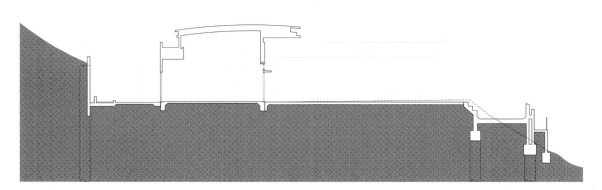

Section BB

The articulated architectural surfaces and geometric forms, along with the groomed landscaping and intentional planting beds, provide a foil to the rocky natural terrain of the cliff and natural vegetation.

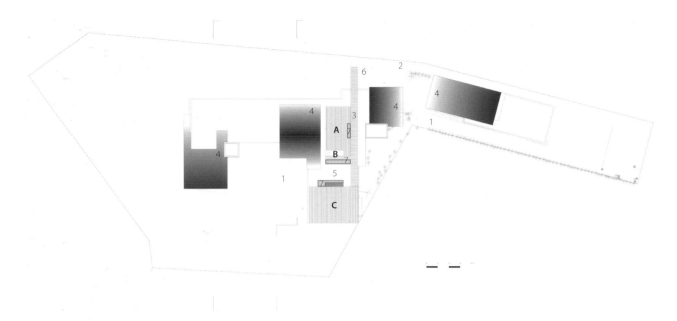

Roof plan

A. Outdoor dining
B. Outdoor bar
C. Outdoor living room

1. Trellis below
2. Retaining wall
3. Wood walkway deck
4. Curved metal roof
5. Skylight
6. Stairs to grade below
7. Planter

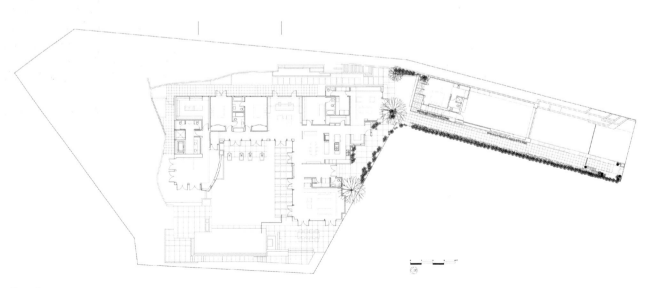

Floor plan

To maximize a large courtyard area off of the main house, a concrete patio and infinity pool elevate and extend out over the cliff's edge.

The transition between interior and exterior spaces is made progressively: more secluded and protected rooms lead to spaces with taller ceilings, skylights, and large sliding glass doors.

SAYRES HOUSE AND HANGING GARDENS

WAINSCOTT, NY, USA

Architect // **Maziar Behrooz Architecture**

Photographer // © **Matthew Carbone**

Not so much an extension of the existing barn, this addition is more of a counterpoint, an op-posite argument. The barn sits foursquare, contained and symmetrical. The addition swings off of one corner, spraying out into the landscape like shards of glass, a landscape, that is likewise fractured into shards—a triangular pool and patios. The counterpoint to the existing barn's basic gable roof are the addition's multi level sod-covered flat planes—plants dripping from the eaves to help integrate the addition closer with its landscape. A central courtyard is bracketed between the staid rectangle of the existing building and exogenic forms of the extension, forming the outdoor room around which the plan is organized.

NEW EXTENSION　　　EXISTING BARN

West elevation

EXISTING BARN　　　NEW EXTENSION

East elevation

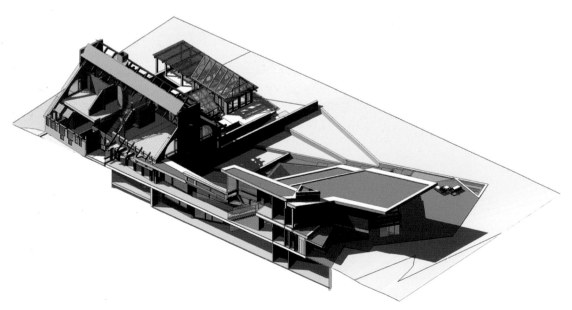

Axonometric view

This home was extended through the creation of two flat, interlocking forms, which, together, host a series of terraces and contrast with the angular nature of the gable roof of the main house.

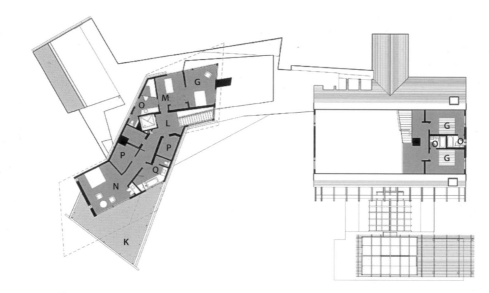

Second floor plan

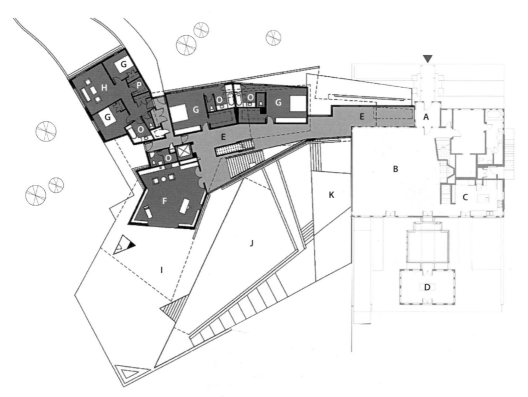

Ground floor plan

A. Entrance
B. Existing living room
C. Existing kitchen
D. Existing dining room
E. Gallery
F. Library
G. Bedroom
H. Caretaker house
I. Patio
J. Pool
K. Terrace
L. Hall
M. Office
N. Master bedroom
O. Bathroom
P. Closet
Q. Master bathroom

Multiple flat roofs at different heights are covered with low-maintenance sedum plants, helping to reduce water runoff and create the impression of a garden on the roof.

The cascading water of the beautiful infinity pool flows as a waterfall over three levels, connecting each floor of the house to the level below.

SUN HOUSE

SINGAPORE

Architect // **Guz Architects**

Photographer // © Patrick Bingham-Hall

Watery surfaces surround you on all sides in this house. Each room and patio is another island in this archipelago of a house. A koi pond fills its central courtyard wall-to-wall, and is separated from a lap pool by just a thin seam. On the other side of the house another pond laps up against the kitchen and study, half submerging them with its surface raised up to the level of the window sills. These water surfaces reflect a dappled light throughout the lofty spaces of the entry and main room, the light filtered first through the site's thick surrounding vegetation and then through vertical wood slats. Green roofs hung with dense plantings hover above this aquatic landscape.

The central courtyard, defined by the L-shape footprint of the house, is dominated by a large fishpond and swimming pool, separated by a hidden seam.

An open terrace with roof garden, situated on the other side of the house, attempts to envelop the aquatic ensemble that is made up of the pond, pool, and large courtyard.

The sense of scale in the courtyard is carefully regulated: the archipelago of parterres and trees that occupies the space is the center of attention.

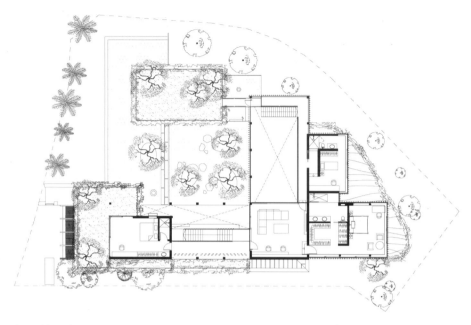

Second floor plan

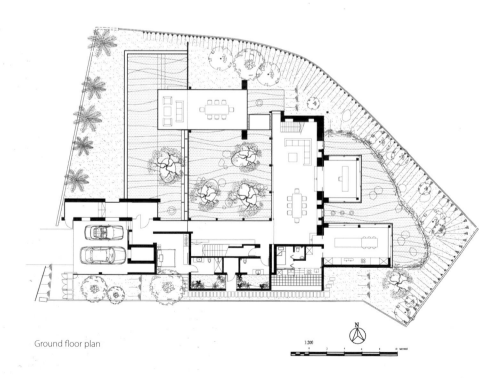

Ground floor plan

1:200

N

CORMANCA
HOUSE

MEXICO CITY, MEXICO

Architect // Paul Cremoux studio

Photographers // © Héctor Armando Herrera and Paul Cremoux

How do you provide greenery for a house on a postage-stamp-sized 12-by-13 meter lot? You landscape the walls. Cormanca House is arranged like a wooden block puzzle. Intricately interlocking voids and solids let air and light right down into the lowest level and allow for a dramatic three-story tall vertical planted wall. A smaller green wall at the back of the site fences in the second level terrace. But the dramatic spaces and vertical garden are not merely an aesthetic statement. They provide the house with natural cooling and ventilation. The vertical garden, with about 4,000 plants, provides major air quality improvements, absorbing over 250 kilograms of carbon dioxide per year and creating a cooling humidity.

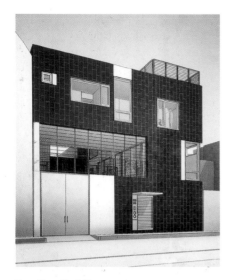

Front view of building

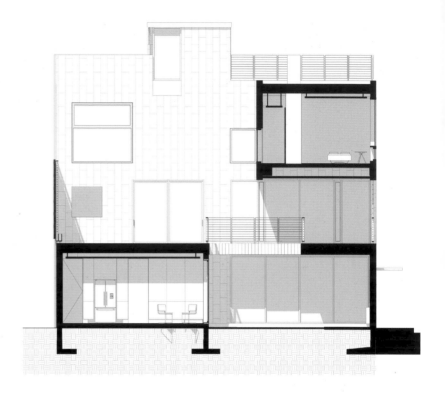

Perspective view of building

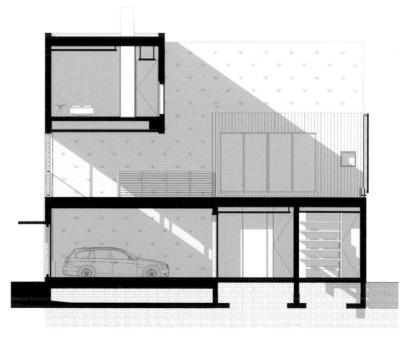

Sections

On a 12-by-13 meter (39-by-42 foot) plot of land, a monolithic volume is transformed into a cluster of interlocked blocks in order to create luminous indoor spaces.

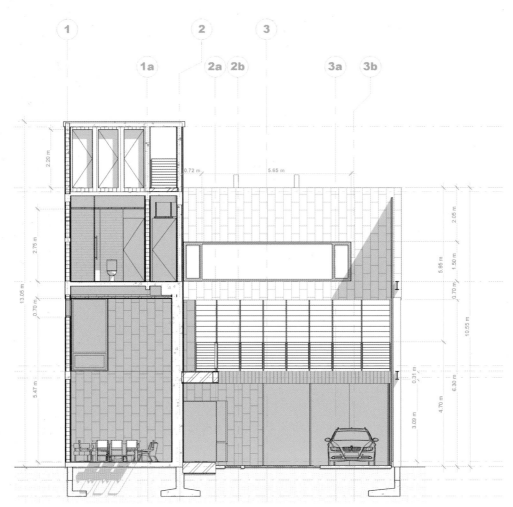

Detailed section

The terrace on the second floor is the main outdoor space for social interaction, since the courtyard on the ground floor is mainly reserved for parking.

Third floor plan

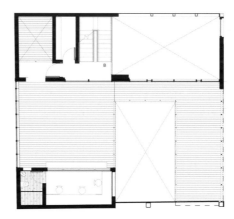

Second floor plan

Ground floor plan

In addition to being a visual attraction, the vertical garden is a major air quality and humidity control device.

VERTICAL GARDEN VILLA CASCAIS

CASCAIS, PORTUGAL

Architect // **Frederico Valsassina Arquitectos**

Landscape architect // **PROAP**

Photographer // © **Frederico Valsassina Arquitectos, PROAP**

Like Cormanca House, this building is composed of an intricate interplay of void and solid carved out of one rectangular solid block. But here, the use of vertical planted walls is not to make up for a lack of green space, as the house sits in a large garden, but to connect the interior spaces with the surrounding landscape. There are three different vertical gardens. Two of them are more exposed to sunlight and are planted with Mediterranean varieties. The third wall receives less light and so has a different variety of plants suitable to its shady environment. The architects have arranged the plantings in finely articulated grids, reflecting the overall parterre of the house.

The landscape architects carefully chose plant species and arranged them using grids, taking into account the general climate of the region, sun and wind exposure, and the specific location inside the house.

PROAP explored the use of landscape for improving the microclimate of an urban environment by introducing vertical gardens, which at the same time enliven the patios and terraces of this villa.

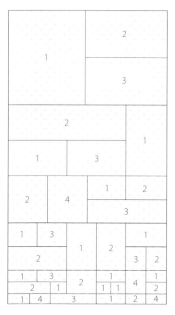

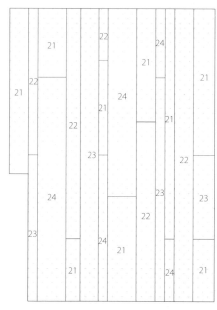

1. *Carex oshimensis* 'Evergold'
2. *Teucrium lucidrys*
3. *Carex comans* 'Frosted curls'
4. *Ceanothus thyrsiflorus*
   'Repens'
11. *Sedum spectabile* 'Iceberg'
12. *Lavandula intermedia*
    'Dutch'
13. *Hebe* 'Emerald green'
14. *Hebe odora* 'New Zealand'
21. *Geranium macr.*
    'Bevan's Variety'
22. *Heuchera* 'Tiramisu'
23. *Luzula sylvatica*
24. *Iris japonica*

Vertical garden composition

HOUSE AT SHIMOGAMO

SHIMOGAMO YAKOCHO, KYOTO, JAPAN

Architect // **Edward Suzuki Associates**

Photographer // © **Yasuhiro Nukamura**

"To be able to see green from every room" was the client's prime directive, and to that end the house is provided with sunny, planted terraces at every level, from the three located at the basement level up to a roof-top deck that takes in longer views of the encompassing neighborhood. These terraces are a parallel set of exterior rooms that correspond to each of the main interior rooms. Translucence and finely modulated screens are the thematic underpinnings of this design. Building on the Japanese tradition of screen walls, the architects used a large variety of these devices to allow the house to be open and light-filled, while still providing privacy on this constricted urban site.

The Interface concept was used to fulfill the client's request to be able to see green from every room and to provide maximum space in a limited area.

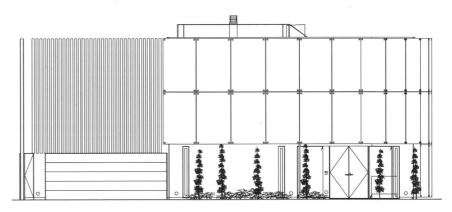

Elevation

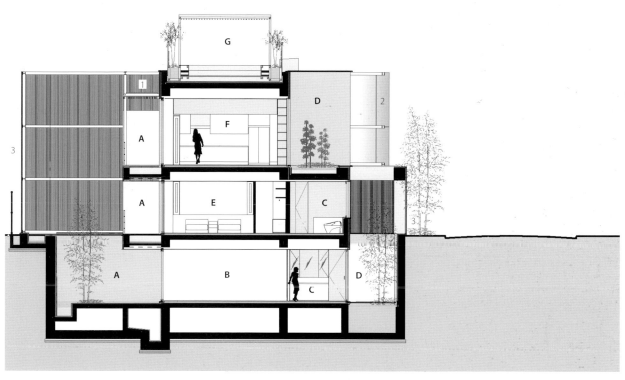

Section

A. Terrace
B. Play room
C. Bathroom
D. Patio
E. Master bedroom
F. Kitchen
G. Roof terrace

1. Louvered glass
   canopy
2. Glass screen
3. Bamboo screen

Interface uses a peripheral screen behind which a green zone is installed. This combination acts as a filter—a buffer zone that enhances communication between inside and out.

Basement floor plan

Ground floor plan

Vertical smoked bamboo blinds are one of the screen types used for the Interface. The other is a circular glass screen that surrounds and protects the second floor on the northeast side.

Second floor plan

A. Patio
B. Japanese room
C. Pit
D. Storage
E. Guest room
F. Play room
G. Study
H. Terrace
I. Garage
J. Storage

K. Entry
L. Foyer
M. Bedroom
N. Master bedroom
O. Walk in closet
P. Living room
Q. Dining room
R. Kitchen
S. Pantry

1. Louvered glass canopy
2. Glass screen
3. Bamboo screen
4. Skylight
5. Glass canopy

HOUSE LIKE
A MUSEUM

KAMAKURA, KANAGAWA PREF., JAPAN

Architect // Edward Suzuki Associates

Photographer // © Yasuhiro Nukamura

A large (15-meter diameter) central round courtyard provides the only connection to the exterior in this very inwardly focused house, as the perimeter walls are windowless and hard up against the boundaries of the site hemmed in by adjacent development. But bands of skylights around the perimeter bring in natural light to help balance the light from the courtyard. The simplicity of the house's sharp white museum like surfaces is reflected in the minimalism of the courtyard landscape, punctuated by one lone tree and a sculptural blob. Despite its internal focus, there is nothing that feels enclosed about the house's airy, light-filled spaces.

The owner's initial idea was that the house should "look to the outside. "The proximity of the neighboring houses and shops led to this idea being abandoned in favor of "looking in."

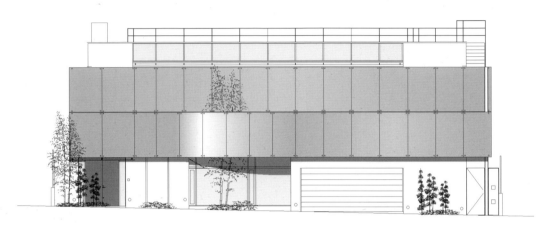

Elevation

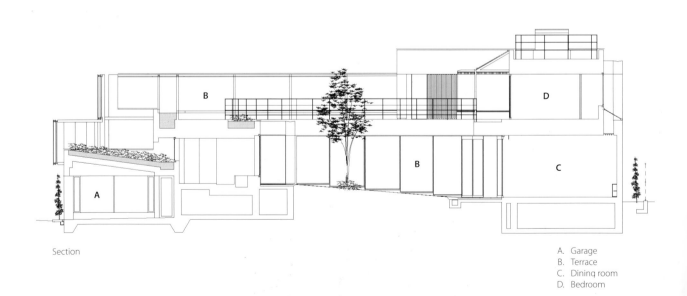

Section

A. Garage
B. Terrace
C. Dining room
D. Bedroom

The rectangular silhouette of the house stretches to the limits of the plot, thereby allowing for a spacious, 15-meter diameter circular courtyard to be located in the center.

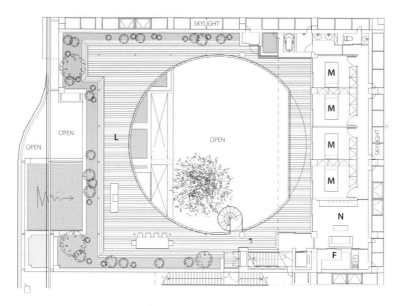

Second floor plan

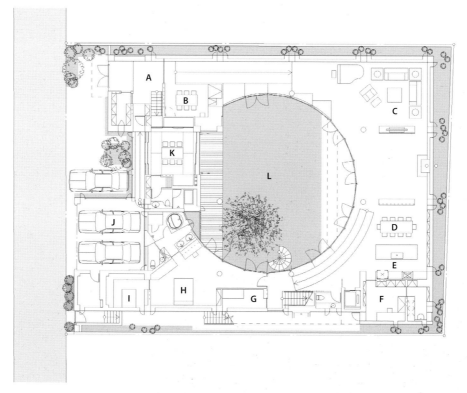

A. Foyer
B. Study
C. Living room
D. Dining room
E. Kitchen
F. Utility
G. Storage
H. Master bedroom
I. Walk-in-closet
J. Garage
K. Japanese room
L. Terrace
M. Bedroom
N. Family room

Ground floor plan

"Go in to go out" is the slogan used in this design. The pivotal idea is to allow each and every room to be orientated toward and have views over the garden.

KRUBINER
RESIDENCE

EMERYVILLE, CA, USA

Architect // Swatt | Miers Architects

Landscape architect // Huettl Landscape Architecture

Photographer // © Russell Abraham

This prefabricated modular house sits on a narrow parcel in a mixed industrial/residential area. Six prefabricated modules are used to make up the home's three bedrooms, three baths, two outdoor terraces, and roof deck. With plenty of sustainable features, this all-electric home is intended to be a net-zero building, producing as much energy as it uses, and, hopefully, to receive LEED Platinum certification. The design makes the most of the limited landscaping opportunities afforded by the site's restricted dimensions, inserting a small green space halfway along the long, narrow plan. Even the driveway was reduced to two narrow tracks of concrete to allow plantings in between.

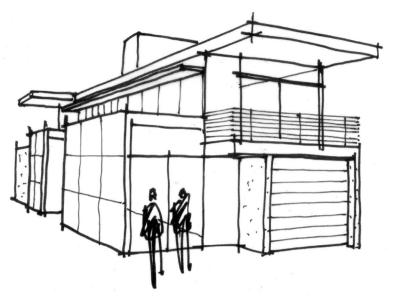

Design development sketch

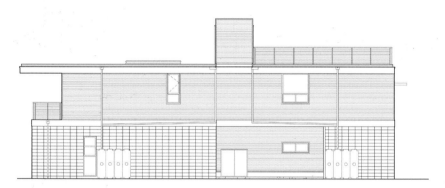

North elevation

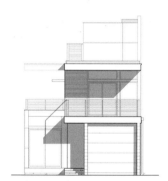

East elevation

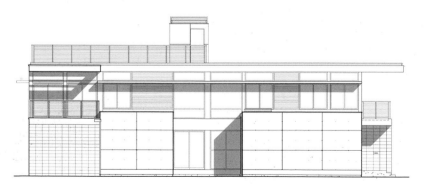

South elevation

West elevation

This two-story home is perfectly suited to the narrow strip of urban land. It is an example of the possibilities and flexibility of the modular Simpatico system.

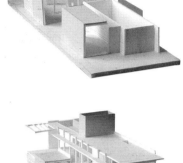

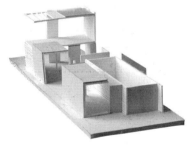

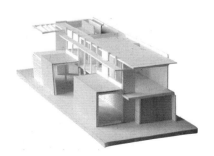

Scale model views

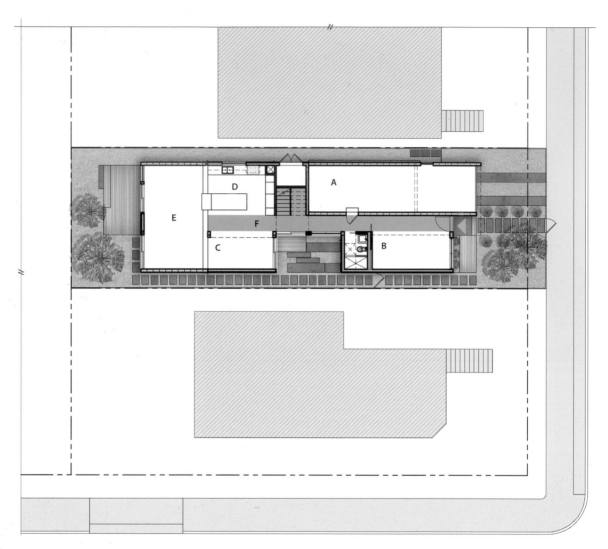

Ground floor plan

A. Garage
B. Den
C. Dining room
D. Kitchen
E. Living room
F. Hallway
G. Bedroom
H. Study
I. Master bedroom

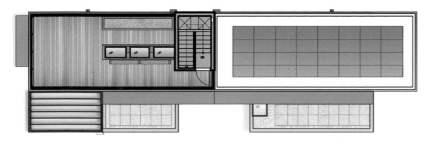

Roof plan

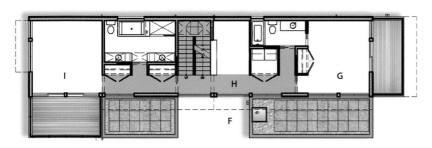

Second floor plan

Passive solar design attracts great visual interest, harnesses natural light, and provides 360-degree panoramic views of San Francisco, Oakland, and Berkeley from the deck.

CHARLES STREET
TOWN HOUSE

NEW YORK, NY, USA

Architect // **Turett Collaborative Architects**
Photographer // © **Turett Collaborative Architects**

This town house, with its clean modern addition, makes the most of its exterior spaces. At the ground level, off the kitchen, is a terrace that is actually the roof of the basement below. Rugged glass skylights integrated into the terrace pavement help light the recreation room below, and also provide up-lighting at night. Midway up the house, another small terrace sits on the roof of the addition, off the master bedroom. The house's last exterior space is at the rooftop, four floors up. Here, a large bank of overstuffed sofas provides an inviting place to relax under the sun. Plantings are limited to planter boxes that run around the perimeter of these spaces, but they provide plenty of green.

In remodeling the building, a beautiful dialogue is created between the ancient and the modern: historic details from a late-nineteenth-century home are preserved, wrapped up in a contemporary casing.

The design of the different terraces of this building is a reflection of its owners' desires: to create spaces with every modern convenience for the family who lives in this historic building.

Front elevation

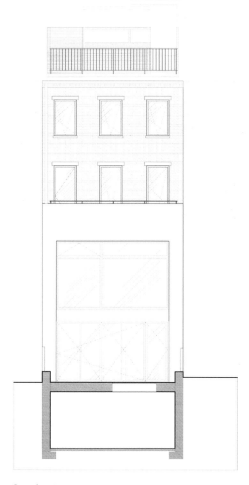

Rear elevation

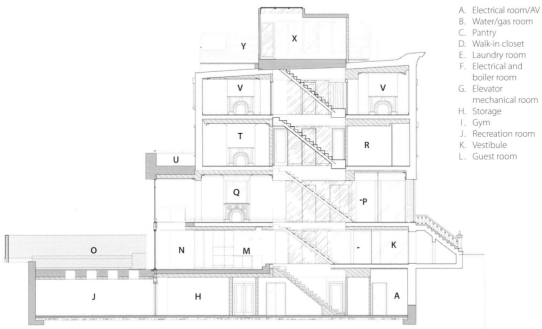

Building section

A. Electrical room/AV
B. Water/gas room
C. Pantry
D. Walk-in closet
E. Laundry room
F. Electrical and boiler room
G. Elevator mechanical room
H. Storage
I. Gym
J. Recreation room
K. Vestibule
L. Guest room

M. Kitchen
N. Dining room
O. Garden
P. Study
Q. Living room
R. Master bathroom
S. Gallery/Closet
T. Master bedroom
U. Patio
V. Bedroom
W. Mechanical deck
X. Roof deck
Y. Roof terrace

Roof plan

Third floor plan

Second floor plan

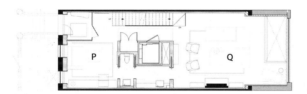

Parlor level floor plan

Garden level floor plan

Basement floor plan

A. Electrical room/AV
B. Water/gas room
C. Pantry
D. Walk-in closet
E. Laundry room
F. Electrical and boiler room
G. Elevator mechanical room
H. Storage
I. Gym
J. Recreation room
K. Vestibule
L. Guest room
M. Kitchen
N. Dining room
O. Garden
P. Study
Q. Living room
R. Master bathroom
S. Gallery/Closet
T. Master bedroom
U. Patio
V. Bedroom
W. Mechanical deck
X. Roof deck
Y. Roof terrace

MURRAY HILL
TOWN HOUSE

NEW YORK, NY, USA

Architect // **SPG Architects**

Landscape architect // **Robin Key Landscape Architecture**

Photographer // © **Daniel Levin**

Originally a two-story carriage house from 1901, today the facade conceals a six-story, 700-square-meter town house on the east side of Manhattan in the Murray Hill neighborhood. The architect's primary task was to remedy the spatial fragmentation that resulted from the numerous renovations. Outdoor space is rare and cherished in New York City. The penthouse of this building allows for indoor/outdoor living, as the adjacent sitting room opens completely onto the terrace in good weather. The magnificent midtown views include the famous Chrysler Building. Although the house is largely detailed in a minimal and modernist manner, Moroccan motifs were used throughout at the client's request.

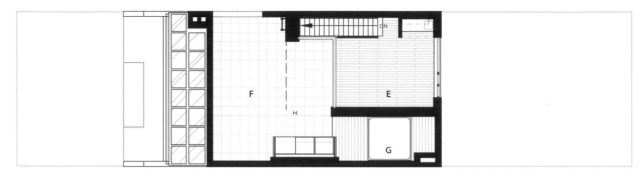

Penthouse upper floor plan

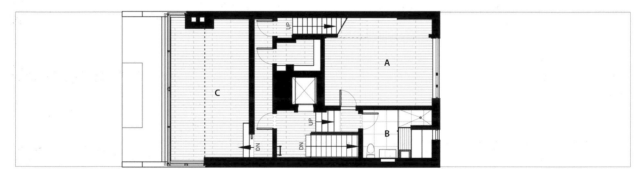

Penthouse lower floor plan

A. Bedroom
B. Bathroom/Sauna
C. Sunroom
D. Elevator
E. Penthouse
F. Penthouse terrace
G. Hot tub

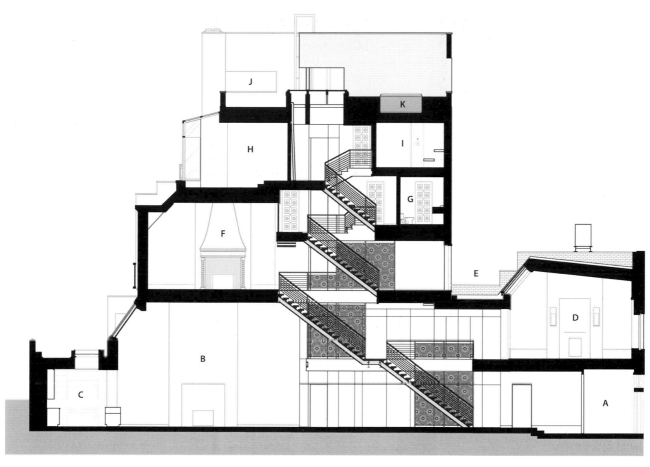

Section

A. Entry
B. Living/dining
   room
C. Kitchen
D. Master bedroom
E. Study terrace

F. Billiards room
G. Bathroom
H. Sunroom
I. Bathroom/Sauna
J. Penthouse terrace
K. Hot tub

BALCONY OF A
PRIVATE HOME

DELFT, THE NETHERLANDS

Landscape architect // **Jos van de Lindeloof Tuin-en Landschapsarchitectenbureau**
Photographers // © **Owner and Jos van de Lindeloof**

Gorgeous detailing and inventive use of materials combine with naturalistic plantings to create a miniriparian habitat in the heart of Delft. From here you have a beautiful view over the historic city center. A long trough provides the water centerpiece of this design, planted with oxygenating plants such as *Pontederia* and "pink swan". The herbaceous borders are planted with high grasses to provide a green shield from the busy cityscape and interposed with flowering perennials. A separate corner is reserved for herbs (such as oregano, sage, thyme, and rosemary). The glass railing provides protection from winds. The deck is finished in recycled plastic planks and polished concrete tiles.

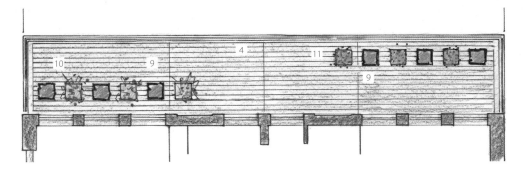

Upper terrace

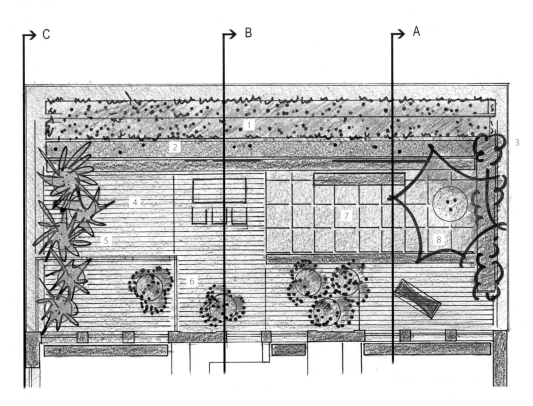

Lower terrace

1. Grass, ferns, and flowers
2. Pond
3. *Rhododendron*
4. Wood deck
5. Bamboo
6. Japanese maple
7. Hard landscape
8. *Koelreuteria*
9. Box
10. *Agapanthus*
11. Grass

The architects' starting points in the design of this terrace were the stipulations laid down by the client: privacy, tranquillity, simplicity, protection from the wind, and a natural feel.

The long pond with sides clad in planed timber draws attention to the width of the terrace. In the central area of the deck, the recycled plastic floor has the appearance of natural wood.

Section A

Section B

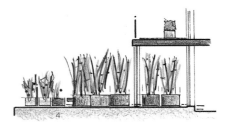

Section C

1. Lounge sofa
2. Step with indirect lighting
3. Table
4. Privacy wall

THE SKY OVER MILAN

MILAN, ITALY

Architect // **Carlo Donati Studio**

Photographer // © **Giorgio Possenti**

This light-filled penthouse sits atop a late-twentieth-century building in the historic heart of Milan. The lower level contains the bedrooms, while the new glass-roofed upper level holds the living spaces. The indoor/outdoor lifestyle is amply accommodated with terraces adjoining every room. The preponderance of glazing at the upper level gives the feeling of actually being outdoors. A central staircase around which the apartment is organized brings natural light down into a sitting room at the core of the lower level. During the day, the Milanese sky is reflected on the windows, while at night a sophisticated lighting system transforms the terraces into a stage.

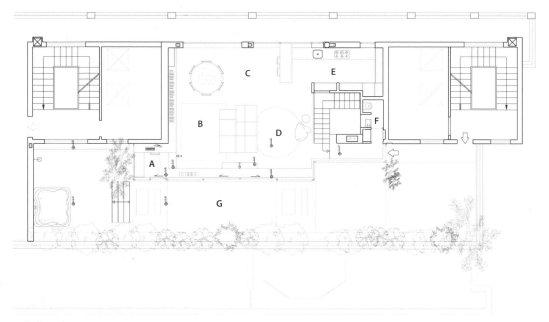

Upper floor plan

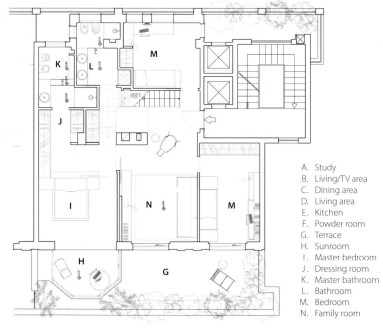

A. Study
B. Living/TV area
C. Dining area
D. Living area
E. Kitchen
F. Powder room
G. Terrace
H. Sunroom
I. Master bedroom
J. Dressing room
K. Master bathroom
L. Bathroom
M. Bedroom
N. Family room

Lower floor plan

The large glass area of this penthouse is a new addition to the building. The light coming through the expansive windows and glass roof floods a spacious living room, which opens onto the terrace.

BIRKEGADE
ROOFTOP
PENTHOUSES

COPENHAGEN, DENMARK

Architect // **JDS Architects**
Photographer // © **JDS Architects**

The addition of three new penthouse apartments on the roof of an existing building provided the opportunity to create a whimsical new roofscape for the building's occupants—a valuable asset for the residents here in the Elmegade district, which is probably one of the most densely populated areas of inner Nørrebro, Copenhagen. A grassy knoll is the central feature, negotiating the change in level between a bright orange upper terrace and a wood-decked terrace one level down. The orange terrace is paved with a shock-absorbing surface for use as a playground. The lower deck is equipped with an outdoor kitchen and barbeque. A viewing platform above the access stair tops off the design.

The garden is designed as a functional space. This is reflected in a playground with shock absorbing surfaces, a green hill, a lookout platform, an outdoor kitchen, and a wooden deck.

Site plan

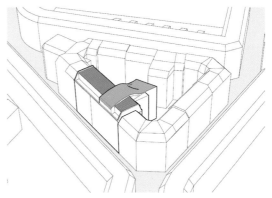

Roof qualities diagram

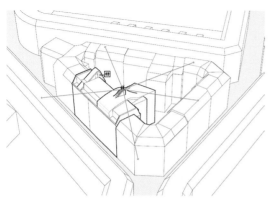

Views diagram

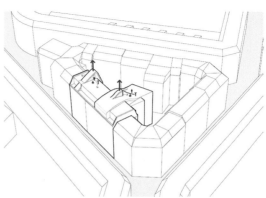

Access diagram

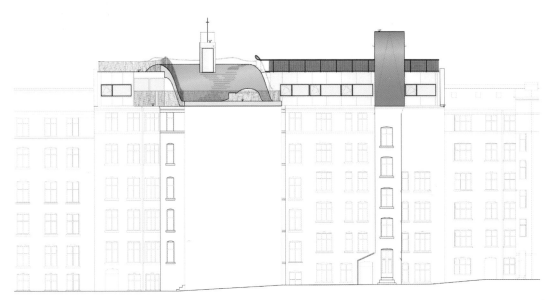

Elevation

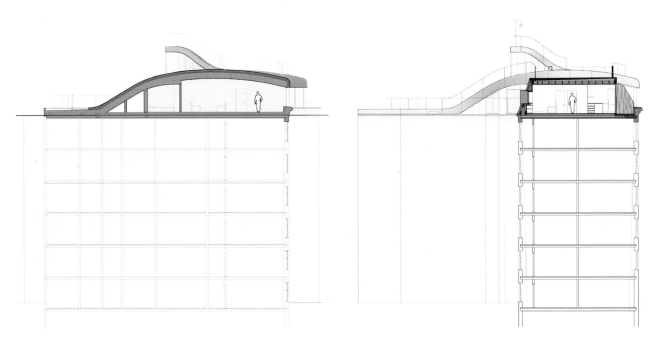

Sections

The construction of three new penthouses on top of an existing residential building in a very densely populated neighborhood of Copenhagen led to the creation of this roof terrace.

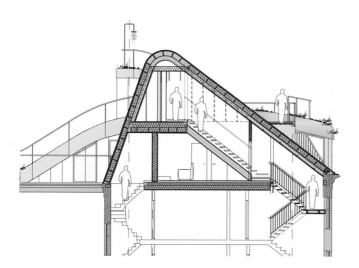
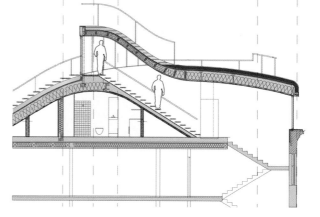

Enlarged sections through penthouses

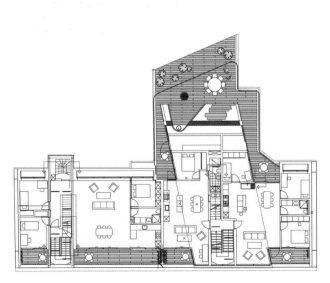

Penthouse lower level floor plan

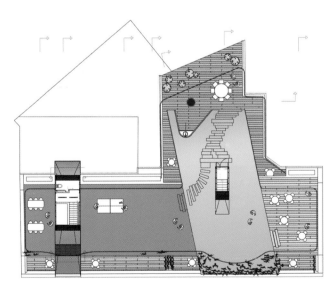

Penthouse upper level floor plan

The beauty of this design lies in the fact that the construction of three new penthouses led to the exploration of ways to make the best use of a rooftop. The aim was to improve the quality of life for the habitants in a densely populated city.

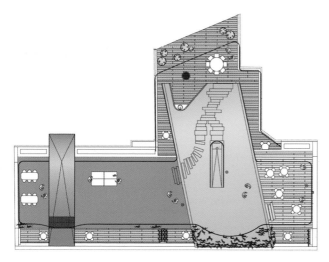

Roof plan

PARKVEIEN 5 B-C

OSLO, NORWAY

Architect // **KIMA Arkitektur**

Landscape architect // **Gullik Gulliksen AS Landskapsarkitekter**

Photographers // © **Finn Ståle Feldberg, Ivan Brodey, and Ragnar Hartvig**

The site consists of a narrow strip of land 7 meters wide and 28 meters deep between two adjacent fire walls, which was in use as the entryway to a power station. The building site was challenging, to say the least, with the tram running less than 3 meters from the facade for 18 hours a day. The main materials are copper and heat-treated pine, with exposed concrete and painted steel. The pine in horizontal slats is a unifying theme running throughout the roof terrace. As the site is completely built-up, the roof became central to providing communal outdoor space. It was turned into a lush garden with public as well as secluded zones. Two of the apartments also have their own private gardens.

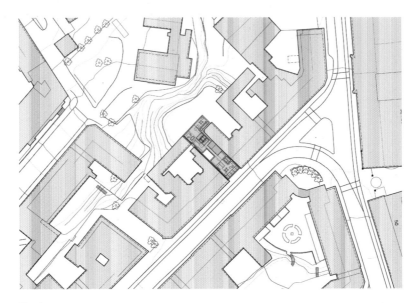

Site plan

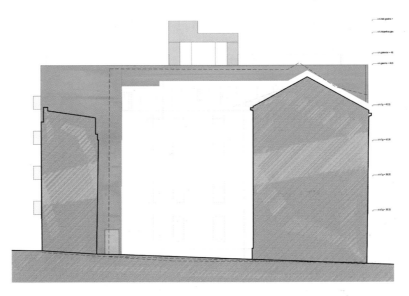

Southwest elevation

The existing conditions of this building prior to its refurbishment limited the possibilities for the creation of open spaces. The adjacent buildings and a ground floor passage to a power station were important constraints.

As the plot is completely filled, the roof became central in order to provide communal outdoor spaces. The result is a lush garden with wide open and secluded zones.

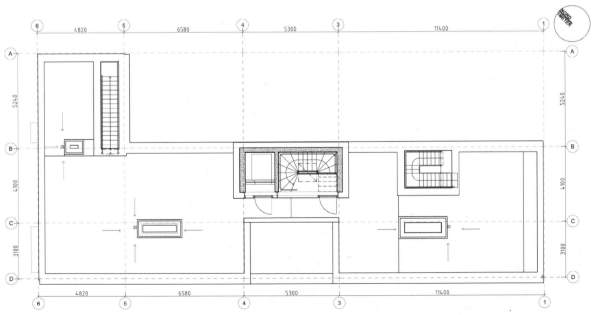

Roof plan

TERRACE IN OVIEDO

OVIEDO, SPAIN

Landscape architect // **Paisaje Norte**

Photographer // © Ramón Álvarez Arbesú

This rooftop terrace completely wraps a penthouse apartment overlooking Oviedo, Spain. Lushly planted with fairly substantial trees, bushes, and lawns, it seems more as if it were a rural garden rather than the top of an apartment block. The brick finish of the existing building is reflected in the use of brick for planting bed borders, tying everything together. A series of circular forms described in the paving materials creates various outdoor "rooms," which helps divide up what would otherwise be very long, narrow spaces. Dense vegetation trained along the parapet fence provides the garden with privacy from the adjacent apartment blocks.

With exposure to the sun as the main design
thread of the terrace, the shade of a pergola, the
freshness of the alternatively arranged plants,
and the lawned zones help to mitigate the ef-
fects of warmer weather.

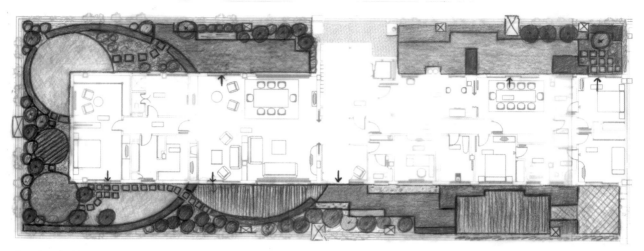

Floor plan

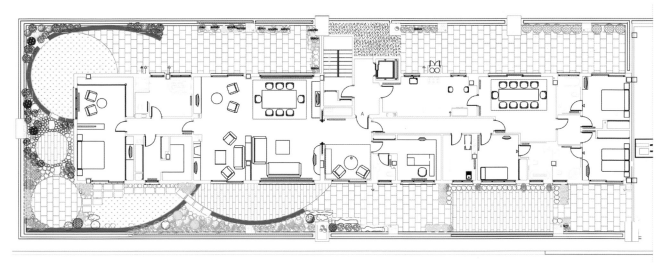

Planting design

	Cornus (pink flower)		Bamboo		*Lavandula*	
	Cornus (white flower)		*Abelia grandiflora* (red)		*Wisteria* (white)	
	Gingko		Tree peony		*Bougainvillea* (pink-orange)	
	Acer or *Cornus* (variegated)		*Choisya ternate* 'Sundance'		*Vitis purpurea*	
	Cercidiphyllum japonicum		*Spiraea nipponica* (white)		*Clematis*	
	Acer palmatum (green-red)		Orange conifer		*Hypericum calycinum*	
	Acer palmatum (red)		*Stipa tenuissima pennisetum*		*Rhododendron* or azalea	
	Acer (green)		Corn		Ferns	
	Betula		*Cotinus*		*Lamium maculatum*	
	Citrus sinensis		*Miscanthus*		*Hosta*	
	Robinia pseudoacacia		*Pittosporum* variegated		*Euphorbia amygdaloides*	
	Tilia		*Abutilon pictum*		*Astilbe*	
	Nandina		*Lysimachia nummularia*		*Hydrangea paniculata* 'Limelight'	
	Bamboo		Mix of bulbs blooming in different seasons		*Hydrangea petiolaris*	

GREENWICH VILLAGE PENTHOUSE

NEW YORK, NY, USA

Architect // SPG Architects

Photographer // © Daniel Levin

This renovation transforms what was a beautiful but austerely minimalist one-bedroom penthouse into a more livable apartment without losing its appeal as a glowing modern space high above Greenwich Village. Its 86-square-meter terrace provides expansive views of New York City and beyond, views that are really the most phenomenal aspect of this terrace. A vivid cerulean blue runs through all the terrace furnishings, complimenting the earth-toned brick, which is the dominant material. All the plantings are contained in pots, giving the terrace a nonchalant and relaxing character.

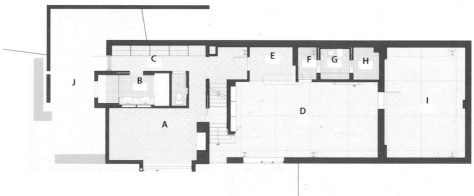

A. Master bedroom
B. Master bathroom
C. Master dressing room
D. Media room
E. Office
F. Media storage
G. Powder room
H. Storage
I. Mechanical room
J. Master bedroom garden

Lower level floor plan

When the horizon is the New York skyline, it ceases to be a screen in the distance and becomes instead a three-dimensional landscape to dive into. Windows are not enough. The terrace is a visual springboard.

ANTONINE
HEIGHTS ROOF
TERRACE

LONDON, UNITED KINGDOM

Landscape architect // **Amir Schlezinger | MyLandscapes**

Photographer // © **Lucy Fitter**

On the borders of Bermondsey and London Bridge, this roof terrace enjoys a truly remarkable panorama of the city, with the recently built Shard towering in the background. This terrace is designed particularly with nighttime enjoyment in mind. Clever lighting tucked into the underside of custom-built planters provides a pleasant low light while a thin light strip marks the line between hardwood decking and sandstone tiles. Strawberry trees, silver birches, and European palms cope well with the exposure at this height. The Western Redcedar screen got a last-minute alteration when the designers realized that the neighbors' view to Canary Wharf would be compromised, so they angled down the end section.

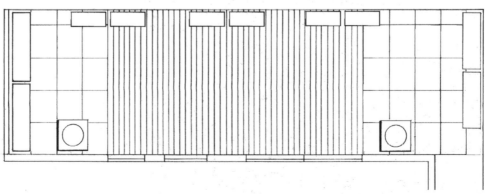

Terrace floor plan

The light strips that separate the sandstone and wood claddings combine perfectly with the lighting of the planters and, in particular, with the night views of the Bermondsey–London Bridge border.

ARTHAUS ROOF TERRACE

LONDON, UNITED KINGDOM

Landscape architect // **Amir Schlezinger | MyLandscapes**
Photographer // © **Lucy Fitter**

This terrace benefits from a sophisticated yet simple design, open and uncluttered. The client, an artist, wanted something creative and colorful yet very low maintenance. While the view to the right had to be screened for privacy, the other sides were kept open to views of the local streets and landmarks. Groupings of custom-designed planters, powder coated in white and various bright colors, populate the terrace. Each contains LED lighting to create a stunning lighting ring effect at night. The two pairs of white circular planters are on movable castors, and each opening at the top is offset to the side, in the mirror image of its mate.

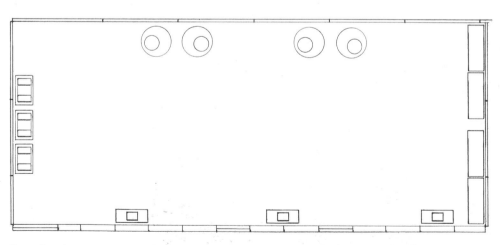

Terrace floor plan

The client who commissioned this terrace is an artist. He wanted a creative and colorful garden that was easy to maintain and sheltered from the communal terrace. Privacy is essential.

ALBERT DOCK
ROOF TERRACE

LONDON, UNITED KINGDOM

Landscape architect // **Amir Schlezinger | MyLandscapes**

Photographer // © **Lucy Fitter**

The minimalist apartment in this converted building near King's Cross had an almost entirely white decor. In keeping with that, the terrace was made as white as possible with white planters, paving, and the trunks of the silver birch trees. The design is dominated by a bowed glass wall arcing out onto the terrace. It enjoys wonderful views of St. Pancras and is surrounded by the canal's water. The smooth sandstone flags are framed by slender sections of hardwood deck on either side, creating two different seating areas. Gaps between the plantings were left to allow one to approach the railing and view the water directly below.

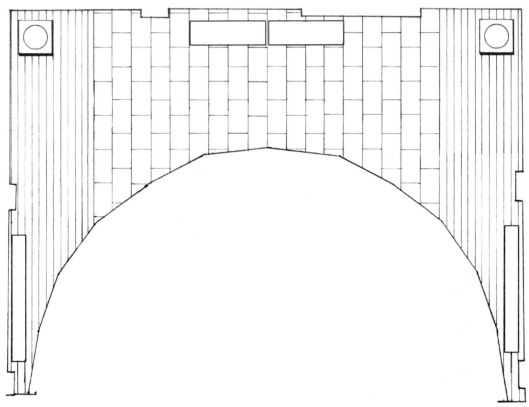

Terrace floor plan

The creator of this terrace, Amir Schlezinger, designs gardens. "He's a bit crazy," says Christopher Fowler, his client. "I wanted to kill him, but then I realized that he was a genius." An artistic temperament.

According to the landscape architect, he was faced with a minimalist building, a refuge from pollution, noise, and urban chaos, even from "aggressive pigeons," he says. The terrace expands this refuge beneath the roofs of London.

URBAN EXTERIOR

MANTUA, ITALY

Architects // **Archiplan Studio**
Photographer // © **Martina Mambrin**

At the top floor of a seventeenth-century building in the historic heart of Mantua, this terrace is at once classical and relaxed. Its symmetrical four-columned pergola has a vaguely Etruscan feel to it with its simple details and clear geometries. The large wooden seat becomes the organizational element as it is used as a shelf for vessels, and candles, and informal seating for a chat with friends. The pergola is covered with a climbing wisteria and the deck is finish in ipe. From the terrace you can enjoy the view over the roofs of the city and the dome of the Basilica of Sant' Andrea, designed in 1400 by the Renaissance architect Leon Battista Alberti.

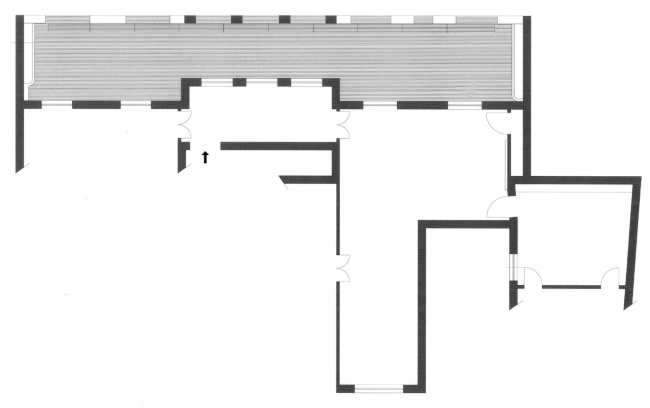

Floor plan

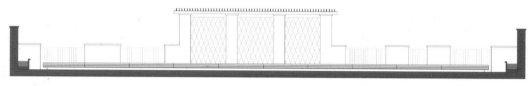

Elevation

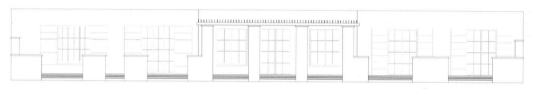

Section AA

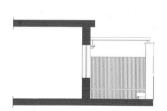

Section BB

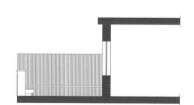

Section CC

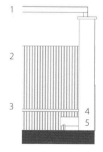

Detailed section

1. Pergola made of 12 x 2 cm
   wood studs, painted white
2. Teak cladding
3. Existing planter clad
   in teak
4. Wood bench
   30 x 2,000 x 40 cm
5. LED lighting

Both the floor and the bench along the edge of the terrace are clad in ipe wood. The bench accentuates the length of the terrace. The pergola, on the other hand, creates a focal area and symmetry.

TERRACE WITH
WATER FEATURE

MADRID, SPAIN

Landscape architect // La Habitación Verde
Photographer // © La Habitación Verde

The designers made the most of this small courtyard, with its elemental water feature composed of the simplest spout possible and a beautiful urn to catch the life-giving flow. A mere 3.5 meters on a side, the terrace contains all that is needed: plants, water, sky, earth, and an indelible sense of place. A nuanced palette of dark and light shades are used in contrast to each other in this charming space. Pale stone paving and the delicately veined light plaster walls are set off by the dark browns of wood, bronzed metal, and ceramic pots, with the greenery providing a third main color element.

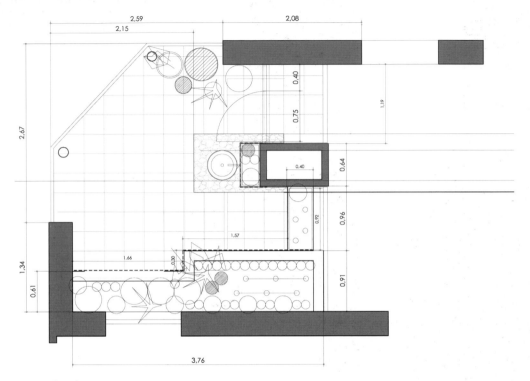

Floor plan

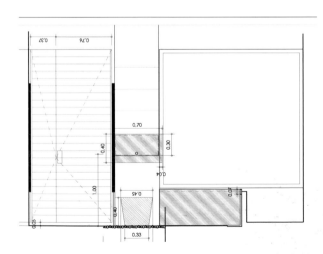

Front elevation at water feature

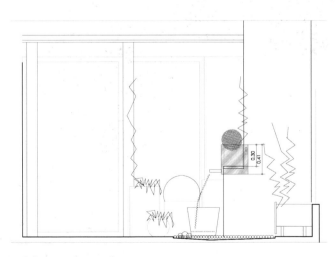

Side elevation at water feature

The design of this interior courtyard creates a beautiful garden with a fountain and refreshing sound of water. It also provides a central ventilation shaft as an integral part of the house.

3/3/2016

5/2016
3c